A History of ACS
The American Community School at Beirut,
1905-2012

Wade H. Morris, Jr.

Cover photograph of Beirut's Corniche and the ACS campus in 1963 by Ray Ruehl

A History of ACS
The American Community School at Beirut
1905-2012

By Wade H. Morris, Jr.

Edited by Patricia Buckley
Designed and typeset by Børre Ludvigsen

Published in Norway by Al Mashriq Publishers for ACS
ISBN 978-82-999320-4-2

Published in Lebanon by Educart (Middle East)
(Paperback ISBN 978-1-941359-03-7)
(Hardback ISBN 978-1-941359-02-0)

14 (on demand)

Students' names are appended with their two-digit actual
or projected date of graduation. Faculty and staff are
identified with (FAC) in the index only.

Available from
The American Community School, Beirut
www.acs.edu.lb
and
www.lulu.com/spotlight/borrel/

Contents

List of Figures

Abbreviations

ACS	American Community School at Beirut
AUB	American University of Beirut (formerly SPC)
Aramco	Arabian American Oil Company
BD	Boarding Department
IB	International Baccalaureate
IC	International College
LB	Lebanese Baccalaureate
PLO	Palestine Liberation Organization
PSP	Progressive Socialist Party
SPC	Syrian Protestant College (now AUB)
Tapline	Trans-Arabian Pipeline Company
UNESCO	United Nations Educational, Scientific and Cultural Organization
USAID	The United States Agency for International Development

Acknowledgments

This book was made possible thanks to the extensive sharing of recollections and insights by a large number of people, only a fraction of whom are mentioned here.

The author's thanks and gratitude go to the following individuals: Maria Abunnasr '84 who shared some primary sources used for her dissertation and who acted as liaison between the author and her mother, Catherine Bashshur during the latter's illness. Sana Yammout in the alumni relations office at IC. Russell LaMont '65 in the New York ACS office. Juliah Smith, Julie Archer and Cheryl Hughes, archivists at Aberystwyth University in Wales. Thanks to Allen West '48, Elisabeth West FitzHugh '43 and David West '51, Jon Stacey '63, Tim Dorman and Pril Dorman Hall, and Quentin Compton-Bishop whose recollections and record enriched this story of ACS. Thanks to Marianne Buckley '80, Haifa Hijazi, Najwa Zabad, Maysa Boubess, Anna Boustany '84, John Nohos '88, Catherine Bashshur and Barea Jawhary whom the author interviewed for this book.

The editor would like to thank Fadwa Ghannoum, director of Development and Alumni Relations at ACS, who has been the guiding force behind the book and who led the project from inception to publication. Barbara Porter '71 and Linda Handschin-Sheppard '68 who provided their advice and guidance in all matters related to this book. Kaoukab Chebaro, Mervat Kobeissi and Samar Mikati, of the AUB Jafet Library's Archives and Special Collections.

Thanks to the individuals who graciously gave of their time to proofread and fact check the manuscript: Allen West '48, Eleanor Dorman Johnson '62, Sam Constan '53, Laila Alamuddin '62, Jeff Hutchins '65, Sara Rich, Valerie Estes Ragan '76, Bill Tracy '53, Melanie Brechtel '72, Marianne Buckley '80, Vaira Harik '83, Ebba El-Hage, Danai El Hajj Ibrahim '06, Farrah Haidar '94, Deirdre Ball '75, Ziyad Ayass '06, Jen McTaggart and Ceci Clark.

Thanks to Børre Ludvigsen '64 who designed and typeset this book, tracked down many of the photographs and prepared the manuscript for publication in Lebanon and online.

- Patricia Buckley

Introduction

The American Community School at Beirut (ACS) has a fascinating story to tell. Born during the Ottoman Empire in 1905, ACS has survived more than a century of catastrophic change and regional conflict. In order to survive, the school has continually adapted and reinvented itself. The story of ACS is a story of resilience.

There are three principal themes or stories told in this book. The first is the school's evolution: the fluctuations in school size, the different levels of parental influence, the increasing complexity of school governance, and – most interestingly – the shifting dynamic between an American identity and a Lebanese identity.

The second is the school's leadership in times of crises. Of particular interest is the leadership of: (i) Margaret Bliss '11 during the famine of the First World War, (ii) Ivy Cleo de Gorkiewicz '35 through the aerial bombings of World War II, and (iii) Clarence Shultz and Jack Harrison in coordinating the evacuations in 1958 and 1967 respectively. Most compelling, however, are the stories of leadership during the Lebanese Civil War. Between 1975 and 1991, Robert Usellis, Elsa Turmelle, and Catherine Carlin Bashshur led the ACS community through daily struggles of survival. This book will attempt to capture the experiences of these leaders and how they persevered during times of great trial.

Thirdly, I hope to tell a narrative story of a living, breathing entity – a school community. As with any school, ACS was and is a collection of its component parts: parents, teachers, administrators, the Board, and most importantly the students. Synthesizing these different and sometimes competing perspectives into a common narrative has been a challenge. I hope that those with a connection to ACS will find some of this narrative familiar and all of the narrative interesting. Those without a personal connection may find ACS's story particularly fascinating and compelling. ACS is a unique institution – due to its mission to provide an American education on the Mediterranean edge of the Middle East – with a unique school community that has lived, and is living, through remarkable times.

To tell the ACS story, I have relied on a variety of sources. First, Jon Stacey '61 collected a series of student and teacher memoirs in 1997, which provided me with a foundation of knowledge for this project. The school's Development Office also conducted and transcribed dozens of interviews in 2004 and 2005, collecting generations of experiences. My interviews filled in the gaps. There is also a series of invaluable primary sources. Letters from parents and students from the early 1910s through the late 1940s reveal much about the first half of the school's history. Beginning in the 1950s, minutes of the Board meetings provide a window into school life. The archives of the American University of Beirut have also been helpful: the personal letters of the university's presidents, the minutes of the university's faculty and Board meetings, and wartime correspondence among university administrators. Their relevance to the greater academic community, including specific references to ACS, helps unlock the story of the school. Finally, ACS's own archives include a wealth of student publications, yearbooks dating back to 1921, photographs, and school newsletters. All of these documents, in their own way, provide the materials for what I hope is a readable narrative.

I went into this project hoping to tell a fascinating story. I leave it with a new perspective on teaching, parenting, the lives of teenagers, and institutional memory. The hundreds of primary sources and interviews led me to a conclusion that may seem self-evident: there was no golden era of the school's past. We should not be nostalgic for a lost period of ACS's history. Letters from the 1920s show us that teachers complained about disrespectful student behavior. Parents fretted over their children's academic workload and unfair grading standards as early as the 1930s. Children always misbehaved – whether dipping a girl's pigtails in ink in 1907, giving a sarcastic blessing at a school dinner in 1938, lighting firecrackers inside the school in 1950, sneaking out through a dorm window in 1965, or abusing drugs in the 1970s. In each decade, students misbehave and adults respond by claiming that the current generation is the worst ever. I find this historical truth comforting.

I hope that ACS's story can, in some small way, give us a perspective on life at ACS today. That perspective should make us proud of the perseverance and character of the school. It should reassure us in facing the current challenges of educating our students. It should give us confidence that this institution, the American Community School, will meet the trials of the future – as long as we allow it to adapt and evolve.

- Wade H. Morris, Jr.

1 The Birth of the Faculty School, 1905-1913

Figure 1.1: Beirut as seen from the Syrian Protestant College c. 1905

Modern-day citizens of Beirut, who are cosmopolitan and connected, would hardly recognize their city in 1905. At the beginning of the 20th century, Beirut was more a chaotic port town than a thriving metropolis. Its population numbered less than 100,000. It was encircled by medieval walls. Its streets were a crowded maze of alleyways – not the paved, grand boulevards of Solidere.[1] Beirut in 1905 had yet to see its first automobile. Oil lamps, not electricity, lit its homes. The city was in a remote corner of the Ottoman Empire, as it had been for nearly 400 years.[2]

Ras Beirut was very much a separate place from the port city just a few kilometers away. It was a rural, village-like area with a few scattered buildings separated by fields of mulberry bushes, citrus groves, and cactus.[3] The center of activity was Rue Bliss, a dirt road that overlooked the Mediterranean. The tallest structure was the minaret of the mosque on the corner of Rue Sadat and Rue Bliss.[4] Aside from the mosque, Rue Bliss had a grocery store, a butchery, and a bakery.[5] It was a quiet, rural area with spectacular views of the Mediterranean.

In the late nineteenth century, a small community emerged on the remote hilltop of Ras Beirut centered around the Syrian Protestant College (SPC). This college, founded in 1863, would be renamed the American University of Beirut in 1920. American expatriate professors and their families mingled with local Muslims, Druze, and Christians living along Rue Bliss. It was within this expatriate community that the American Community School, then called the Faculty School, was born. The American families associated with SPC wanted a distinctly American-style education to prepare their children for universities in the United States. Because such a school did not exist in Beirut, they felt compelled to create one.

Figure 1.2: The Syrian Protestant College campus at the time of president Howard Bliss's arrival c. 1903

An Informal Event: Creating the Faculty School

The idea of creating a Faculty School began in November 1903 when Howard Bliss, the second president of SPC, arrived on campus. Earlier that year, the College's Board of Trustees had unanimously selected Bliss to succeed his father as president. Arriving with Bliss that November were his wife, Amy Blatchford Bliss, their four children (a fifth would be born in Beirut), and a young woman named Miss Winifred Thornton.

Figure 1.3: Rue Bliss at the turn of the century

The Blisses had hired Winifred Thornton while in England en route from New York to Beirut. Thornton had graduated from Aberystwyth University in Wales the year before, receiving a degree in "Intermediate Arts."[6] She was in her early twenties when she arrived in Beirut, where she was initially employed as a "governess" to educate the Bliss children.[7]

Lessons were given in Marquand House, the residence of SPC presidents. Within a few months, children from outside the Bliss family began attending Thornton's informal classes.[8] By the spring of 1905, the Dormans, children of a doctor and dean of the Medical Faculty at SPC; the Moores, children of a doctor; and the Wests, children of a mathematics and astronomy professor, were all crowding into Marquand House for Thornton's lessons.[9] What became the American Community

Figure 1.4: Faculty School students describe walking along "cactus lanes" on
their way to school each day

School grew out of the rapidly increasing and enthusiastic demand for
Thornton's classes.

In the spring of 1905, SPC families held three meetings to discuss trans-
forming Thornton's classes into a school. A few dozen parents attended
these first informal meetings. These parents selected three leaders to
form a committee to prepare a detailed proposal for the new school:

> *Professor West took charge of the drawing up of a curriculum*
> *and a list of textbooks. Dr. Moore was to make inquiries*
> *regarding [a location for the school], and Mrs. Bliss was to*
> *act as a Secretary.*[10]

Essentially, these three parents were the founders of what became the
American Community School. They combined their talents in the summer of 1905 to realize the needs of an expatriate community for a functioning school.

Robert West was the intellect of the committee. West arrived in Beirut
in 1883, and he spent more than twenty years at SPC serving as a mathematics and astronomy professor, principal of the Preparatory Department, director of the observatory, and treasurer. By 1905, West was dean
of SPC.[11] He was an academic with decades of experience in managing

4

Figure 1.5: The Medical Gate of the Syrian Protestant College, 1900

professors and students alike. He was therefore well suited to the primary academic tasks in creating the Faculty School with a particular focus on the curriculum for the new school.

If West had the brains, Dr. Franklin Moore had the muscle of the committee. Moore was a former Princeton athlete and was described as energetic and assertive.[12] He was also the founder of the Women's and Children's Hospital at SPC, and that experience made him well suited to the organizational and business challenges of creating an entirely new institution. Moore found a schoolhouse to rent, set the tuition, and chaired the meetings that planned the school.

Amy Blatchford Bliss, the wife of SPC's president, was the heart of the committee. Her 1941 obituary emphasized her "friendliness, quiet humor, and common sense" as a "constant service to all who came in contact with her."[13] Of the three founders, Bliss held the longest tenure at the school. Decades after the founding of the Faculty School, Bliss was still involved with recruiting faculty and raising funds for the school.

On June 5, 1905, West, Moore, and Bliss proposed a plan for the school to prospective parents at a "town meeting" at Marquand House. Under the proposal, the curriculum would follow, as closely as possible, "the course of study of American public schools." The initial location of the school would be the Boghossian House, on the first floor of the

Figure 1.6: Robert Haldane West and Franklin Thomas Moore

Dorman home on Bliss Street. Three teachers would be employed: Mlle Clemence Imer for instruction in French, a second teacher whose name has been lost, and Winifred Thornton. Thornton, who already knew many of the pupils, would also act as the principal of the Faculty School. The tuition was about $80 a year.[14] The parents in attendance agreed to the plan. Thus, on June 5, 1905, the Faculty School was founded.[15]

The creation of the Faculty School was a low-key event. The committee wrote a constitution (which has not survived) but did not apply for a charter from the U.S. Embassy, local government officials, or even from the Syrian Protestant College. While the founding parents were entirely College faculty and their spouses, there was no formal relationship at this early stage between the Faculty School and SPC. The College's Board of Trustees, which met in New York City every year, did not mention the Faculty School in their minutes until 1920.[16] With the benefit of hindsight, June 5, 1905 was a momentous event in the history of ACS. At the time, however, it seemed of interest only to those involved.

Despite the fact that his wife was deeply involved in the founding and daily operations of the school, Howard Bliss, the president of the Syrian Protestant College, did not appear to take an active role in the Faculty School. In Bliss's surviving letters, he never mentioned Thornton, his children's education, or the creation of a new school. This does not mean that he was an absent or disengaged father. People who knew Howard Bliss described him as a wonderful and caring father. His lack of

6

Figure 1.7: Amy Blatchford Bliss with her husband Howard in Marquand House

focus on the Faculty School in his letters probably reflects his attention to the challenges of managing SPC. From the outset, neither the SPC Board of Trustees nor its president took an active role in the management of what would become the American Community School at Beirut.

The School on the "Little Dirty Lane"

The Faculty School remained in the Dorman residence on Bliss Street for only a year. For the second year, Dr. Moore arranged for the school's relocation to the building across from SPC's Medical Gate next to the Women's Hospital. The building was a one-story stone structure that originally served as a nurses' dormitory. Three Ottoman-style windows hung over the doorway, with barred windows spaced along the sides of the building. A mud-brick wall surrounded the schoolhouse which created a courtyard for recess. There were two or three fruit trees inside the courtyard which were used as bases during games of tag. A wall separated the Faculty School from the hospital.

The only known photograph of the first schoolhouse gives the impression of a dusty, hot space. Students passed through groves of cacti on

7

Figure 1.8: The only known photograph of the Faculty School's first school-house located across from SPC's Medical Gate

their way to and from the schoolhouse.[17] That road was a "little dirty lane, [with] muddy pools of water," wrote one early pupil. "People used to throw garbage and dead cats [in the road outside the school]. We used to call it Stink Lane."[18] The schoolhouse was eventually torn down in 1971.[19]

The Winifred Thornton Years

Winifred Thornton was the undisputed leader of the Faculty School. The 1906 photograph of faculty and students shows a very youthful Thornton sitting in the center. She was in her mid-twenties when she oversaw the responsibility for twenty children and two other teachers.[20]

Some students recalled Thornton as a disciplinarian. Belle Dorman '25, who began first grade at the Faculty School in 1914, remembers being intimidated by Thornton. Thornton's pince-nez glasses were particularly horrifying for Belle, and they caused her to cry on the walk to school each morning. Belle also remembered Thornton's system of order marks, where the "slightest infraction" was recorded and then collected in monthly reports that were sent home to parents.[21] Another student, Rachel Hall '23, remembered Thornton as a woman of "very strict principles." Each week, Thornton made students stand in rows in order of monthly academic averages. This was a practice that Rachel, who typically stood at the end of the row, hated.[22]

Figure 1.9: The Faculty School's first year, 1905-1906. Winifred Thornton at the right, middle row

On the other hand, there is evidence that Thornton was much more than a disciplinarian. The 1921 yearbook, published six years after she left Beirut, states that Thornton "received [students] with great kindness."[23] Even the frightened Belle Dorman wrote that Thornton was "a kindly and precise Englishwoman, a teacher remembered fondly by those who knew her longer than I."[24] Thornton was the one constant adult presence in the first decade of the Faculty School. In the 1906, 1910, and 1914 school photographs, Thornton is the only teacher present in each picture.[25] She was the glue of the school and her students respected her for her constancy.

Reading, Religion and Recess

The Faculty School opened its doors to 18 pupils in 1905.[26] At age twelve, Margaret Bliss '11 was one of the older students, although Margaret remembered having even older classmates at different points of time.[27] During the early years, the Faculty School was primarily an elementary school. As the years passed, additional students enrolled and existing students graduated to high school. While students in the 1906 school photograph appear quite young, the 1910 and 1914 school pictures have teenagers standing in the back row, towering over the younger children seated below.

Enrollment climbed steadily from 1905 to 1914. By 1908, the school had 31 pupils. The 1910 photograph shows 46 students seated around four teachers. Belle Dorman remembered well over forty students when she began in 1914.[28] The Faculty School was growing. The children of SPC professors were staying longer in Beirut instead of attending boarding schools in the United States, and the children of American missionaries increased the enrollment as time progressed. Several students remember these children, unaffiliated with SPC, boarding in their homes during the school week. By the mid-1910s, the school had grown beyond its original purpose of educating only SPC faculty children.

Figure 1.10: The 1910 Faculty School student body and teachers

Religion was a daily presence in the early years of the Faculty School. Students memorized Bible verses each week.[29] Each day began with a hymn sung by the entire student body, and the schoolhouse served as Sunday school on the weekends.[30] One of the few written references that SPC President Howard Bliss made about the Faculty School was how much he enjoyed the school's Thanksgiving choral concert during a 1907 church service.[31] The focus on Christianity was natural given that the Syrian Protestant College began as a missionary school and that the children of missionaries attended the Faculty School.

However, most of the written memories of the students revolved around unregulated time. Belle Dorman recalled having her pigtails dipped in an inkwell by the boys sitting behind her.[32] As for Archie Crawford '18, his fondest memories were of recess. "A fifteen minute recess," Archie wrote, "would leave you absolutely streaming with sweat as you returned to your desk and tried to concentrate on geography or French."[33] Rachel Hall '23 spent her recesses jumping rope. Donkeys wandering outside classroom windows or into the school courtyard added to the excitement of break time.[34]

The Faculty School, later renamed the American Community School, would go on to face major challenges over the course of a century. The first was the famine of World War I.

Notes

[1] Khalaf [2006, pp. 75-76]; Dodge [1958, p. 37]

[2] Kassir [2010, p. 158 & 302]

[3] Khalaf [2006, p. 66]

[4] Dodge [1958, p. 38]

[5] Hall [2001, p. 6]

[6] Aberystwyth University [2011]

[7] Tracy [1989, p. 22]

[8] Stacey [1997, p. 13]

[9] Leavitt [2011]; In the letter, Margaret Bliss Leavitt '11, Howard Bliss's daughter, mentions the West children attending Thornton's classes at Marquand House.

[10] Leavitt [1972b]

[11] Dodge [1958, p. 22]

[12] Board of Trustees of the Syrian Protestant College, "In Memory of Dr. Franklin T. Moore.", January 26, 1915 (3/7)

[13] Obituary [1941]

[14] Leavitt [1972b]; Most of what we know about the founding of the Faculty School comes from this letter. Margaret Bliss Leavitt '11 was one of the original eighteen students at that school, was the daughter of Howard Bliss, and was the first graduate of the Faculty School in 1911. In 1915, she returned to Beirut after University and taught at the Faculty School for the remainder of the First World War. The 1972 letter outlines the meetings and the key people involved in creating the Faculty School. Leavitt addressed it to Wilfred Turmelle, an ACS teacher and administrator at the time. While the letter was dated 1972, the summary of the school's history has a 1949 date. Leavitt may have written the history 23 years earlier. The letter also cites and quotes from the original minutes of those first three meetings as well as from the original founding "constitution" of the school. Presumably, Leavitt had access to those documents in the late 1940s. Those documents, however, have since been lost. One can assume that the original minutes and founding constitution were kept by Margaret's mother, Amy Blatchford Bliss, who acted as secretary. These records may have been passed on to her daughter after her death in 1941. The whereabouts of these founding documents are now unknown.

[15] Leavitt [1972b]

[16] Board of Trustees of the Syrian Protestant College, January 30, 1902 through July 14, 1921 (3/1-9)

[17] Stacey [1997, p. 11]

[18] Crawford [1972a]

[19] Crawford [1972a]

[20] 1906 Faculty School Photograph, ACS Archives.

[21] Rugh [1991, p. 1]

[22] Hall [2001, Part I - Early Years, p. 8]

[23] ACS [b, 1921]

[24] Rugh [1991, p. 1]

[25] 1906, 1910, 1914 Faculty School photographs, ACS Archives.

[26] Tracy [1989, p. 22]

[27] Leavitt [1972b]

[28] Rugh [1991, p. 1]

[29] Hall [2001, Part I - Early Years, p. 9]

[30] Rugh [1991, pp. 1-2]; Hall [2001, Part I - Early Years, p. 14]

[31] Bliss [1907]

[32] Rugh [1991, pp. 1-2]

[33] Stacey [1997, p. 13]

[34] Stacey [1997, p. 11]

2 The First Crisis, 1914-1920

Figure 2.1: SPC campus and Ain el Mreisseh on the eve of the First World War

The First World War had a devastating impact on Beirut. This in turn posed great challenges for the Syrian Protestant College and the Faculty School. Most seriously, the war threatened the health of every child, teacher and parent within the Faculty School, and it claimed the lives of several.

The First World War in Beirut

The Ottoman Empire went to war with Russia, Great Britain, and France on October 28, 1914, at the beginning of the tenth year of the Faculty

School. British and French citizens living in Beirut were the first to feel the war's impact. Howard Bliss, president of the Syrian Protestant College wrote in October that the "British missionaries are leaving."[1] Later that fall, the Ottoman government closed British and French schools and confiscated their properties.[2] By December 1915, "orders came that all members of British and French communities were to be deported inland."[3]

Events then led to a man-made disaster. First, the British and French navies began their blockade of Beirut's once thriving port. Bayard Dodge, who at the time was the director of West Hall and would later be a Faculty School parent, described British cruisers off the coast of the College firing over ninety shells into Beirut.[4] The blockade, an attack of locusts, the severe winter of 1915-1916, and the Ottoman Empire's inept rationing of food all combined to create a famine that devastated Beirut. The journalist and historian Samir Kassir describes "weeks when dozens of deaths were recorded each day, sometimes as many as two hundred."[5] The American consul in Beirut recorded in July 1916 that Beirut's streets were "filled with starving women and children… In my early evening walks I frequently see people lying dead in the gutter."[6]

Historians have debated the total number of civilians killed in Lebanon and Greater Syria as a result of World War I. Bayard Dodge and his daughter Grace Dodge Guthrie '32, who were members of the Faculty School community, put the number of dead at 300,000.[7] The estimates of professional historians are even higher. William Cleveland claims that 600,000 civilians living in what is now Lebanon, Syria, Palestine, and Jordan died from 1915 to 1918.[8] Elizabeth Thompson, another historian, estimates that famine, disease, and combat killed 18 percent of the pre-war population of Lebanon. That figure dwarfs the proportion of casualties in Europe. Five percent of the prewar populations in France and Germany died as a result of the war.[9]

War and the Syrian Protestant College

As president of the Syrian Protestant College, Howard Bliss became the *de facto* leader of the small community of Americans living in Ras Beirut – and, as a result, he was indirectly responsible for the well-being of the Faculty School. If SPC closed its doors, then the Faculty School, without its sponsor, would close also. Bliss therefore deserves credit for saving not only SPC but also the Faculty School.

When the war broke out, SPC had to overcome declining enrollment, a shortage of teachers, and a lack of funds. As early as 1915, the SPC

14

Board of Trustees, meeting in New York City, debated whether to close the school due to the loss of students to Ottoman conscription.[10] Bliss avoided a school closure by convincing Ottoman officials to give hundreds of his students exemptions from military service.[11] After all, Bliss argued, SPC educated future doctors, lawyers, and engineers of the empire. To offset declining enrollment, Bliss borrowed money. From 1914 to 1917, SPC accumulated $510,258 of debt while it graduated just twenty-nine students in 1917.[12]

While Turkey and the United States never officially declared war on each other, in April 1917 the United States did enter the war on the side of Britain, France and Russia. The American community in Ras Beirut subsequently came under the close scrutiny of Ottoman officials, and on April 22, 1917, the Ottoman governor of Beirut closed SPC for ten days.[13] To reopen, the College was required to pay a special tax, its curriculum was monitored, and it was forced to teach the Turkish language for the first time. By the summer of 1917, Americans were anticipating deportation into the interior of the Ottoman Empire, as the British and French had been in 1915.[14] The deportations never occurred although the threat led to another wave of voluntary emigration in the summer of 1917.

The war progressed and increasing numbers of Americans fled Beirut. Bliss's letters throughout the war years lament the departure of one colleague after another. One letter describes the College campus as "eerily quiet" – despite the commotion of war in the surrounding area.[15] Many American families who left Beirut took with them pupils from the Faculty School. By 1918, just twenty-five American families remained within the College community.[16]

In order to survive, SPC maintained cordial relations with Ottoman officials. The College volunteered its medical staff for the Empire in 1915, and Jemal Pasha, the regional governor of Greater Syria, seemed grateful to Bliss for the services that SPC had given him.[17] Jemal Pasha and Bliss became acquaintances, and the Ottoman governor made several visits to the campus, where he was received with the "utmost friendliness."[18] On March 22, 1917, nearly three years into the war, Bliss wrote that, "We had a very delightful visit from His Excellency Muhammad Jemal Pasha."[19] Later in November 1917, Bliss again met with Jemal Pasha, who had "recently come to Beirut, and I had a pleasant call upon him." Bliss added, "I hope he will come to the College on his next visit."[20]

Bliss's ties to the Ottoman government may have given the College community, and by extension the Faculty School, special access to food rations.[21] Bliss made an indirect reference to these privileges in an October 1917 letter, stating that "the government continues to show us many kindnesses and we hope that we shall be able to show that we deserve them."[22] His cordial relationship with Ottoman officials has since been a source of controversy – especially in light of Jemal Pasha's responsibility for the public execution of eleven Arab nationalists in 1916 in Beirut's Bourj, which has since been renamed Martyr's Square. Many Lebanese also blame Jemal Pasha for the devastation of the famine, although his level of responsibility is debatable. When Jemal Pasha left Damascus in 1918, he was known across Greater Syria as "Al-Saffah" – the Blood Shedder.[23] Nevertheless, by providing extra rations, the Blood Shedder may have helped SPC, and with it the Faculty School, to survive.

After overcoming the hunger, disease, debt, enrollment decline, and political pressure of World War I, Howard Bliss became a casualty of the war. In 1919, Bliss's health declined rapidly. He was diagnosed with diabetes, presumably a result of wartime malnutrition. In the spring of 1920, Bliss struggled with pneumonia and then succumbed to tuberculosis on May 2. The College newspaper wrote, "Dr. Bliss's unexpected death at the age 59 was a direct result of the strain which he endured during the war."[24]

Figure 2.2: Howard Bliss (front row, first from left) with officers of the Ottoman Army, including Jemal Pasha (front row, center)

War and the Faculty School Leadership

Few existing primary sources refer to the Faculty School during the war. There are no known photographs of students and faculty from 1914 to 1918. What remains are Bliss's passing references to the Faculty School in private letters as well as student memories recorded decades later.

Despite the shortage of sources, we do know that Winifred Thornton, the founding principal of the Faculty School, left Beirut in 1915 due to the conflict. Thornton, unlike most of the faculty and students, was British, and of course Britain had been at war with the Ottomans since October 1914. She therefore most likely registered with other British residents in November 1914.[25] The Ottomans had issued several orders for the deportation of all citizens of belligerent nations, the first in June 1915. One can therefore assume that Thornton, would have been deported sometime in 1915 had she not fled.[26] Her students, however, never forgot her. In 1921, the graduating seniors of the Faculty School dedicated the first yearbook in school history in her honor.

Margaret Bliss filled the vacuum left by Thornton's departure. Margaret was the daughter of Howard and Amy Bliss and the first graduate of the Faculty School in 1911. After graduating from Vassar College, Margaret returned to Beirut in 1915 to teach at the Faculty School. Howard Bliss wrote to his brother at the time that "Margaret finds her work here very agreeable in the Faculty School." Bliss then added, "Of course, there are not so many pupils this year as in the past."[27] A Faculty School parent wrote at the end of the war that "[Margaret] has been fine these past few years carrying all the burdens of the school and now that she has gone [the burdens] fall back on the Committee [of parents]".[28] Margaret appears to have been the only full-time teacher at the Faculty School from 1915 through 1918.

The parents of children attending the Faculty School significantly contributed to the school's survival. The summer of 1917 was exceptionally difficult for the American community in Ras Beirut. The Faculty School lacked pupils. With the exception of Margaret Bliss, there were no full-time English-speaking teachers. With wartime inflation, the cost of living skyrocketed. There were shortages of textbooks as well as food. Parents met on June 5, 1917 to discuss closing the school. According to Margaret Bliss, at that meeting "a number of the parents and others in the community volunteered their services to help out."[29] Five mothers and fathers taught various subjects, including French, history and mathematics.[30] The evidence suggests that the Faculty School managed to remain open throughout the war thanks to the leadership of Margaret Bliss and the active support of the school's parents.[31]

Student Experiences during the War

When Harry Dorman '22 reflected on his experiences during the war, he was surprised that he could not remember the devastation caused by the war. He was the son of a doctor in the medical school and was just fourteen when the war ended. He did not recall the starvation and disease that are now part of the historical record. "[The lack of memories] gives an idea of how completely, as kids, we were sheltered by our parents from what was going on around us," Dorman wrote. "We kids were not taken downtown, where dead bodies were sometimes lying on the sidewalks, where beggars or even ordinary people starved to death."[32] Separated from the heart of Beirut, the American families were able to isolate themselves from the most horrific scenes of the war.

Huntington Bliss '21, the son of SPC's president and a year older than Harry Dorman, also seemed sheltered from the war. He wrote that during the war "our food was strictly limited in variety but adequate in amount." But Huntington did not mention seeing others starve. His memory of the attack of locusts in 1915, which devastated crops in Greater Syria, was one of boyish playfulness. "I was in Sunday school looking out of the window to the south," Huntington recalled. "I noticed that the bright sky was suddenly covered by a dark moving cloud. The locusts had arrived. After Sunday school, I hurried home, grabbed my tennis racket, stood at the north end of our tennis court and batted them as they came along."[33]

Despite their relative safety in Ras Beirut, several students at the Faculty School did record observations of wartime suffering. One of the early memories of Grace Dodge '32 was of her father working in several soup kitchens that fed 800 people in the area around Beirut.[34] She later played with and tutored Armenian orphans, who were abandoned in Beirut as refugees.[35] Similarly, the Hall family consciously exposed their children to the suffering. Years later, Rachel Hall '23 wrote:

> *My parents felt that my brother and I (age twelve and ten) should see firsthand what was happening, so we spent one weekend hiking in the mountains with my father, visiting the soup kitchens. I remember the beauty of the mountainside, and the smell of the pines in the hot sunshine. I also remember clearly a small boy with his tin bowl coming along*

the rough path to the kitchen for his portion of lentil soup, stopping to lick up from a rock a little of that soup that someone had spilled.

Even at the age of ten, Rachel was aware of "the starving villagers, crawling down to the city looking for food. Family groups camped out by the side of the road where we walked to school." She adds, "We knew that a death cart came through each morning to pick up the dead. And I have a very vivid memory of those starving people with their dark hollow eyes, and the children lying in rags, with distended bellies, too weak and sick to get up."[36]

Figure 2.3: A group of volunteer nurses from the Syrian Protestant College Expedition to Auja al-Hafir; Dr. Ward (far right) was a Faculty School parent.

Parents could not protect their children from some experiences, such as the illness or death of a community member. In January 1915, the Faculty School lost one of its founders when Dr. Franklin Moore died at the age of 44. His death came as a shock to those who knew him. With a body weakened by overwork and exhaustion, Dr. Moore succumbed to what may have been typhoid fever.[37] His death devastated Moore's wife and five children, all of whom were members of the Faculty School community.[38] Harry '22 and Belle Dorman '25, the children of a doctor at SPC, nearly lost their father to malaria. In the spring of 1917, Howard Bliss did not expect Dorman to live[39]. "Dr. Dorman," Bliss wrote to an SPC trustee, "is still at the Hospital where he is very ill and apparently just holding his own. Mary Dorman [Dorman's wife] requests that nothing should be said to Dr. Dorman's mother."[40] Fortunately, Dorman recovered, and Bliss's letters chronicle his slow return to health.

Tragically, a child within the American community, Dorothy Patch, died of malaria in September 1917 just prior to her sixth birthday. "On Tuesday she seemed perfectly well but a very severe attack of pernicious malaria set in and she died on Wednesday afternoon," Bliss lamented.[41] At age six, she would have begun classes at the Faculty School. Her death was a result of the malnutrition and disease rampant during World War I.

War's End ...

The British army entered Beirut on October 8, 1918, thus ending the war for the city.[42] This occurred a week after the fall of Damascus, and the Turks did not attempt to defend Beirut. Huntington Bliss '21, a Faculty School student, played soccer with British officers and invited a few home to the Marquand House for dinner.[43] The war had finally ended for the two dozen or so American families who remained in Ras Beirut.[44]

Yet the Faculty School still had obstacles to overcome. One of the daughters of Howard Bliss suffered some sort of mental breakdown – probably what we now call post-traumatic stress disorder.[45] Edward Nickolay, the interim president of SPC after Bliss's death, reported "sporadic cases of the plague" immediately after the war.[46] In 1920, Nickolay complained of a lack of housing for two Faculty School teachers, the first new full-time teachers since Margaret Bliss. He described a meeting in which Faculty School parents once again pulled together for the benefit of the school, this time allowing the new teachers to live in their homes without charge.[47]

Despite the post-war obstacles, by 1920 the Faculty School emerged stronger than ever. Enrollment was once again on the rise and by 1920, it was higher than it had been in 1914.[48] Other small schools in the area catering to foreign missionaries had closed due to war and famine.[49]

The school relocated from the old building next to the hospital to a larger building just off Jeanne d'Arc Street, donated by Amy Blatchford Bliss, one of the founders and the widow of President Howard Bliss.[50]

The parents rewrote the school constitution in 1921 to include the Protestant Mission as a second "sponsor." That document renamed the school the American Community School at Beirut.[51]

ACS had survived one of the greatest humanitarian disasters in the history of Beirut and had established itself as one of the leading primary and secondary American-style educational institutions in the Middle East. It became increasingly integrated with the larger community of expatriates in Greater Lebanon and Syria.

As a result, ACS would no longer be run by a close-knit group of parents. It would never again be so closely affiliated with the Syrian Protestant College, which in 1920 was renamed the American University of Beirut (AUB). The school now had a Boarding Department, new teachers, a new campus, athletic teams, and a music department.[52] Many families unaffiliated with AUB sent their children dozens – or hundreds – of miles to attend the expanding school.

Notes

[1] Bliss [1914]

[2] Penrose [1941, p. 150]

[3] Penrose [1941, p. 152]

[4] Dodge [1958, p. 43]

[5] Kassir [2010, p. 245]

[6] Thompson [2000, p. 20]

[7] Dodge [1958, p. 46];Guthrie [1984, p. 17]

[8] Cleveland [2004, p. 154]

[9] Thompson [2000, p. 23]

[10] Board of Trustees of the Syrian Protestant College, January 26, 1915 (3/7)

[11] Penrose [1941, p. 152]

[12] Dodge [1958, p. 50]

[13] Crawford [1972b, p. 24]

[14] Bliss [1917g]

[15] Bliss [1917f]

[16] Obituary [1920b]

[17] Crawford [1972b, p. 23]

[18] Ward [1915]

[19] Bliss [1917a]

[20] Bliss [1917b]

[21] Crawford [1972b, pp. 23-24];Penrose [1941, p. 154]

[22] Bliss [1917e]

[23] Cleveland [2004, p. 154]

[24] Obituary [1920a];

[25] Ward [1914]

[26] Penrose [1941, p. 152], Penrose gives December 1915 as the date for the deportation of British faculty at SPC.

[27] Bliss [1917h]

[28] Ward [1920]

[29] Leavitt [1972b]

[30] Ward [1920]

[31] Leavitt [1972b]

[32] Stacey [1997, p. 13]

[33] Stacey [1997, p. 6]

[34] Guthrie [1984, p. 15]

[35] Guthrie [1984, pp. 22-23]

[36] Hall [2001, Part I – Early Years, p. 16]

[37] Board of Trustees of the Syrian Protestant College, January 26, 1915. (3/7)

[38] Penrose [1941, p. 155]

[39] Dr. Harry Gaylord Dorman, 1876-1943, practiced pediatrics and physiology at the SPC/AUB hospital from 1903.

[40] Bliss [1917d].

[41] Bliss [1917c]

[42] Thompson [2000, p. 39]

[43] Stacey [1997, p. 6]

[44] Guthrie [1984, p. 81]

[45] Guthrie [1984, p. 84]

[46] Nickolay [1919]

[47] Nickolay [1920]

[48] Hall [2001, Interim – The War Years, p. 1]

[49] Leavitt [1972a];Crawford [1972a]

[50] Crawford [1972a]

[51] Leavitt [1972a]

[52] Rugh [1991, p. 1]

3 A New Identity, 1921-1939

Figure 3.1: The American Community School's first brochure, 1921

Beirut was in post-war shock. Greater Lebanon was now under the French Mandate. Wartime naval bombardments had left neighborhoods in ruin. The medieval alleyways that survived the war were demolished in favor of a city-plan of wide, straight avenues modeled on the boulevards of Paris. These cultural and structural changes were accompanied by the physical and mental effects of the famine.[1] In the first few years after the war, 10,000 children were hospitalized and 140,000 adults received intensive medical care.[2]

Despite these conditions, the population of Beirut doubled between 1921 and 1931. With the increase in population came growth of businesses. The number of hotels in Beirut nearly doubled in the 1920s, as did the number of insurance companies, doctors, architects, and engineers.[3] Before the First World War there were only six registered automobiles in Beirut; in 1921, there were 372; by 1931, there were more than 10,000.[4] In four years, 450,000 square meters of roads and sidewalks were paved.[5] Shantytowns arose, filled with Armenian, Syrian, and Egyptian refugees.[6] Prior to the war, foreigners represented five percent of Beirut's population. Soon after the war, foreign residency rose to 15 percent.[7]

Meanwhile, Ras Beirut continued to be dominated by gardens, small farms, and a few villas.[8] The neighborhood lacked the infrastructure of a functioning city and still seemed independent from the city of Beirut. One ACS student in the 1920s described Ras Beirut's "ditches that ran down both sides of the road carrying the sewage off to the sea."[9]

The American Community School, like Beirut, reinvented itself after the First World War.

The New Mission: Serving a Region of Expatriates

In 1921, ACS did something that it had never done before: it advertised. ACS parents developed a pocket-sized pamphlet to recruit students from beyond Ras Beirut. The pamphlet stated that "[We] are working, as you to share the best in our national [American] genius: the spread of free principles, the release of the spirit of education, and the guidance of life in Jesus." The audience was the regional community of American missionaries and diplomats. American children in the Middle East, the pamphlet explained, were "growing up more familiar with camels than with automobiles, or with the daily voice of muezzin from the mosque than with the weekly church bells." The pamphlet promised the "Americanization of Americans."[10]

The student population thus began to change. The Faculty School had always promised to give its pupils an American-style education and to prepare American children for universities in the United States. In 1921, the parents in charge of ACS expanded enrollment by creating a Boarding Department. American families from as far away as Cairo and Tehran entrusted their children to the school. Instead of serving the families of a small community, ACS now served a wide community of expatriates. The simple public relations campaign paid off. The school grew from barely a dozen students during World War I to 43 in 1924, and to 69 in 1933.[11]

The New Campus: The Look and Feel of a School

ACS also had a new campus in a three-story building off of Rue Jeanne d'Arc, two blocks south of Bliss Street.[12] The building was surrounded by dirt lanes and cactus fields, far from the urban landscape that one sees in the 21st century.[13]

The schoolhouse was L-shaped. The ground floor served as an assembly hall with classrooms. The second and third floors served as a cafeteria, recreation space, and residence rooms for the Boarding Department.[14] Girls lived on the second floor and boys on the third. Three arched windows hung over the main doorway, leading into a central room that served both as an auditorium and the library.[15] A six-foot sandstone wall surrounded the dirt schoolyard.[16]

In its first fifteen years, the school had rented a former nurses' dormitory from AUB. Now, for the first time, ACS had its own facilities. As the 1920s progressed, rooms were added for science classes and a stage was added for performances.[17] The Boarding Department on the second and third floors underwent several renovations. ACS now looked like a school.

Parents: Loosening of Control

From 1919 through the mid-1920s, parents operated the school on a daily basis. They did so through a "Committee" of parents in charge of securing funds, acquiring land for a new campus, hiring teachers, and writing new policies. The Committee then reported to all ACS parents, known as the "Association," through town-hall style meetings. The Association then voted on specific initiatives. The school, quite literally, was run by parental committee subject to parental democracy.

Hiring new American faculty was a particular challenge for the parents. Amy Blatchford Bliss returned to the U.S. to recruit teachers in the

Figure 3.2: The American Community School campus from 1921 through 1949

wake of World War I, but she failed to find a single teacher willing to move to Beirut.[18] Over five years later, parents were still volunteering as teachers to meet the needs of the school.[19] By the late 1920s the efforts to recruit American faculty began to pay off. "It is really quite thrilling to have applicants [for faculty positions] come to us," one member of the Committee wrote in 1927. "For all the years that I have been connected with the Committee we have had to draw upon teachers ourselves, and now to have four or five – no six – teachers offering themselves to us seems too good to be true."[20] American teachers were finally eager to live and work in Beirut.

In addition to recruiting faculty, the Committee set school policies, and policy decisions required constant negotiation, compromise, and consensus building. Major and minor decisions were voted on by the parents (the "Association"), which became a painstaking and frustrating process. For example, Charlotte Ward, the leader of the Committee, had to persuade the Association to adopt a French curriculum.[21] When a tenth grader wanted to drop her history class in favor of Greek, the parent-led Committee had the final say.[22] The Committee also oversaw every detail concerning the new school building, from the color of the window frames to the height of the ceilings.[23] Increasingly, the volunteer Committee became a full-time job.[24]

For over a year, Charlotte Ward considered quitting the Committee. "I could almost wish that I was off the Committee, even though I am greatly interested in the school work," Ward explained. "I dread working in

Figure 3.3: Charlotte Ward, a leader of the Parent Committee in the mid-1920s, was charged with running the daily operations of the American Community School. She is pictured here with her children, c. 1918.

another Committee."[25] When she finally resigned in 1927, Ward wrote that "it is getting on my nerves to interview parents with criticisms, others whose children are refused admission, or to be responsible for the teachers."[26] The Committee had taken on the tasks of professional, full-time school administrators.

After creating a small family-run school in 1905, and after volunteering to run the daily operations of the school during World War I, ACS parents finally handed control to a professional administrator, Violet Bender, in 1927. Bender was the school's first official principal since Winifred Thornton departed in 1915. Ward immediately recognized the difference that Bender made:

> *It is such a comfort to have Miss Bender take hold of things at the school. She seems firm and keen-minded and not only does the Committee feel the difference in being able to leave much of the school business to her but the children and the*

*parents feel it in the way school goes. We think that we are
going to be very happy to have her as principal.*[27]

Bender's hiring marked a shift in the history of ACS. As the 1930s progressed, the school grew away from the tight parental control that marked the first twenty years of the school's history. ACS was growing up.

A More Modern School

Prior to the First World War, the Faculty School had focused on reading, writing, and arithmetic. Full-time teachers had taught French and Latin, but volunteer parents had taught science. There had been no visual arts, no drama productions, and no music classes other than singing hymns. There had been no physical education classes or organized team sports. By the mid-1920s, all of that changed, and extracurricular activities became a focus of the ACS experience.

Music and art, in particular, became part of the weekly routine. Fine arts classes met four times a week, twice for visual arts and twice for music. The last period on Friday afternoons was reserved for non-academic programs, which allowed students to demonstrate their musical talents.[28] The choir was particularly popular, using the same "wonderful green songbook" used by many public schools in the United States.[29] Students formed a school orchestra with the help of the faculty of AUB, and its first official performance was during the 1925 graduation ceremony. "We didn't know we were all that important until we saw our names in the program," one student wrote about the event.[30]

Beginning in 1930, ACS had a stage on which to perform musicals and plays. Shakespeare was especially popular. Students spent weeks preparing for productions of *The Merchant of Venice* and *A Midsummer Night's Dream.* "The costumes were dandy and they were mostly patched together with the things we could find," one student wrote in a letter home.[31] One teacher even choreographed a student dance. "Hilarious hours were spent learning the intricacies of the traditional Maypole dance," remembered a student, "the bigger boys muttering and grumbling through the daily rehearsals."[32]

Physical education also became part of the school's weekly routine. There were mandatory calisthenics class in the school courtyard every Tuesday and Thursday and after-school sports teams for the first time.[33] Margaret Merrill '26 joined the field hockey team in 1925 and "got banged up" while still having "loads of fun."[34] Anne Byerly Moore

Figure 3.4: Students on a mountain field trip, early 1920s

'40 "played first base and was a forward on the girls' basketball team, sporting a made-to-order uniform."[35] For boys, "baseball is all the rage," as one student wrote in 1926. "The boys play all the time before and after school recess and as long as the sun is out."[36] Games became social events for the entire school community. To encourage attendance, parents gave away sandwiches and free ice cream.[37] The school, however, did not have dominant teams. ACS competed against schools with older, larger students and quickness did not always make up for the deficit in size.[38] Regardless of wins and losses, sports were now part of the school culture.

The New Faculty: Leaving a Life-Long Impression

Rhoda Orme, originally a Latin teacher, replaced Violet Bender as the school's principal in 1932, and she served in that capacity until 1940. As the Latin teacher, Orme demanded excellence. Her students devoted about an hour each day to memorizing 50 lines of Virgil, and they complained regularly about the work load.[39]

Orme's administrative style seemed similar to her style as a Latin teacher. She was organized, meticulous, and demanding. But the students acknowledged that she cared about them.[40]

29

Figure 3.5: Rhoda Orme (fifth from left, second row) and Olga Holenkoff
(seventh from left, second row), 1930

Bruce Billings, a biology and math teacher, was one of the teachers under Orme's supervision. He was tall and lanky and would perch on the corner of his desk while delivering lectures on the different parts of plants.[41] He was also "loads of fun," as one student described, happy to digress from the content for the sake of a good joke or funny story.[42] Billings' classes went beyond lectures. He challenged his students to engage with science as his students experimented with rats, chased paramecium under a microscope, and made charts of mitosis.[43] He also led field trips to the Beirut River to collect samples of aquatic life – an activity that is not an option in the 21st century.[44]

Perhaps the most beloved member of the ACS faculty throughout the 1920s and 1930s was Madame Olga Holenkoff, a French teacher. Holenkoff was Russian. Her family fled the Bolshevik Revolution and ended up in Beirut.[45] Holenkoff also was a dedicated member of the broader school community. She volunteered to choreograph student performances and musicals. She organized an all-school "French picnic" at the Dog River.[46] She attended each play and athletic competition, all while donating her time to help organize school dances; "she is almost always the chaperone," one student wrote in 1925.[47] Above all, Holenkoff loved her students, and she exchanged letters with them years after

Figure 3.6: Boarding students, 1928

they left Beirut. "She was a delightful lady," Mary-Averett Seelye '35 stated over sixty years later.[48] Almost every primary source from the 1920s and 1930s mentions her, and she was praised in nearly every interview with students from the period.

Life in the Boarding Department

The American Community School added its Boarding Department in 1921. By the mid-1930s the department included several dozen children whose parents lived across the Middle East. This included Elizabeth Kuenzler '36, whose parents were Swiss missionaries working in Turkey. There were the four Cochran girls, whose father was an American missionary in Tehran. Bill Nute '34 came from Turkey, and the Merrill sisters from Aleppo. There were children whose parents worked in Damascus, Palestine, Cairo, and Baghdad.[49]

Boarding students lived on the second and third floors of the school building. A dorm mother resided on the second floor. Dorm rooms housed three or four students but the center of activities was the living room on the second floor or what was sometimes referred to as the community lounge.[50] "There were games, tables to play on, and a bookcase full of books," one student remembered of the living room.[51] This living room filled the hours of down time. Ping-pong, for example,

31

Figure 3.7: The Class of 1929 on graduation day

became "all the rage" in 1937.[52] Impromptu dance parties erupted at night in the community lounge, with teenagers teaching themselves the foxtrot, the waltz, and the rumba.[53]

Boarders developed close bonds – of both affection and irritation. Betty Witherspoon '37, made friendships that were "everlasting" and her time there "was the happiest I have yet known."[54] Children helped one another overcome their homesickness, as older boarders took the younger ones under their care.[55] They shared each other's germs as well.[56] Outbreaks of the flu, measles, and occasionally typhoid fever were just some of the side effects of children living together in close quarters.[57] In the 1930s, a social clique of girls, self-named the "Miraculous Club," hurt the feelings of the girls who were excluded.[58]

Swimming in the Mediterranean provided an opportunity for students to escape the confines of school. "Staff Cove," situated just below the lighthouse, was the most popular swimming hole. The girls were able to change clothes behind the rocks, and Staff Cove was a prime spot for octopus hunting.[59] For the new kids without experience swimming in the Mediterranean, the water seemed choppy.[60] The more experienced swimmers navigated the water dashing against the rocks with ease.[61] But swimmers were humbled by the mini-tsunami that hit Staff Cove in 1934. Without much warning, a wall of water slammed into approxi-

Figure 3.8: ACS students enjoy Staff Cove

mately 25 students swimming at the time. The wave suddenly raised the students several meters and then just as quickly dropped them onto the rocks. Then, the wave receded into the Mediterranean taking with it all of the clothes left on the shore. One word described the effects of the tsunami: "Pandemonium!"[62]

While swimming entertained students during the day, formal dances kept boarders busy on weekend nights. The dances were exciting and unprecedented in the 1930s, yet they bore little resemblance to 21st century high school dances. Each dance was hosted by a student, or group of students, and took place either at school or in someone's home. They were organized, strictly chaperoned events. The program typically included a list of songs and corresponding dances.[63] Boys had to sign up with dance partners by initialing a girl's program next to the corresponding song.[64] One dance in 1939 was particularly "rowdy" because the sign-up system broke down when boys began "cutting in" in the middle of songs. The chaos created some embarrassment when teenage girls were left standing alone as their dance partners wandered off to find other dates.[65]

In 1939, boarders revolted against the dorm mother, Miss Matthews. From the students' perspective, the new, stricter policies of Matthews provoked the rebellion. As the year progressed, girls refused to wear the required knee-high socks, boys rolled their eyes during nightly pray-

33

ers, and evening hymn singing was boycotted. One young lady openly talked back to Matthews when asked to finish her homework before supper.[66] Boys and girls conspired to stay up past lights out and they rotated duties to look out for the approaching matron. The insurrection culminated when three boys refused to go to church, resulting in a week-long suspension. As further punishment, they were required to live with local ACS families. When they returned to the Boarding Department, they looked "meek as lambs."[67]

The life in the new Boarding Department was transformative for the boarders. It also reshaped the school as a whole into a fuller and more dynamic community.

In the two decades after the First World War, the ACS carved out a new role for itself as a boarding school that was among the leading American-style secondary schools in the Middle East. ACS offered its students experiences that resembled those of schools in the United States. From 1921 to 1939, ACS became what we now would recognize as a modern school community. By implementing these changes, ACS had developed the institutional strength necessary to survive the second great trauma of the 20th century: World War II.

Notes

[1] Kassir [2010, p. 266]

[2] Khalaf [2006, p. 76]

[3] Kassir [2010, p. 267]

[4] Kassir [2010, p. 303]

[5] Kassir [2010, p. 286]

[6] Kassir [2010, p. 296]

[7] Thompson [2000, p. 178]

[8] Khalaf [2006, p. 84]

[9] Brown [2006, p. 18]

[10] ACS [1923]

[11] Stacey [1997, p. 17]

[12] Tracy [1989, p. 23]

[13] FitzHugh; Seelye [2004].

[14] Constan [2005]

[15] Compton-Bishop [1996]

[16] Stacey [1997, pp. 17-18]

[17] Stacey [1997, p. 19]

[18] Ward [1920]

[19] Merrill [1925a]

[20] Ward [1923a]

[21] Ward [1923a]

[22] Merrill [1925f]

[23] Ward [1923c]

[24] Ward [1923b]

[25] Ward [1926a]

[26] Ward [1927]

[27] Ward [1926b]

[28] Stacey [1997, p. 22]

[29] Stacey [1997, p. 30]

[30] Merrill [1925c]

[31] Merrill [1925d]

[32] Stacey [1997, p. 32]

[33] Stacey [1997, p. 23]

[34] Merrill [1925e]

[35] Stacey [1997, p. 31]

[36] Merrill Dorman [1926]

[37] Compton-Bishop [1996]

[38] Stacey [1997, p. 33]

[39] Merrill [1925e]

[40] Stacey [1997, p. 31]

[41] FitzHugh

[42] Cochran [1937-1939, p. 11]

[43] Cochran [1937-1939, pp. 14, 16, 19]

[44] Cochran [1937-1939, p. 36]

[45] FitzHugh

[46] Compton-Bishop [1996]

[47] Merrill [1925g]

[48] Seelye [2004]

[49] ACS [1923]

[50] Stacey [1997, p. 25]

[51] Stacey [1997, p. 21]

[52] Cochran [1937-1939, p. 23]

[53] Cochran [1937-1939, p. 8]

[54] Stacey [1997, p. 16]

[55] Stacey [1997, p. 30]

[56] Merrill [1925b]

[57] Cochran [1937-1939, pp. 58-59]

[58] Merrill [1926]

[59] Brown [2006, p. 25]

[60] Compton-Bishop [1996]; Merrill [1925a]

[61] Cochran [1937-1939, p. 2]

[62] Stacey [1997, p. 25]

[63] Cochran [1937-1939, p. 8]

[64] Cochran [1937-1939, p. 40]

[65] Cochran [1937-1939, p. 62]

[66] Cochran [1037-1939, p. 44]

[67] Cochran [1937-1939, p. 35]

4 ACS and the Second World War, 1939-1945

Figure 4.1: Ain el Mreisseh in the early 1940s

The first reaction of Beirut to the outbreak of the Second World War was fear. Those over the age of 25 remembered the famine in the First World War.[1] Beirut braced itself for a repeat of those horrors.

While the famine did not reoccur, violent conflict came to Beirut. June and July 1941 witnessed a bizarre moment in the war: Vichy France, allied with Germany, fought against the Free French forces, allied with Britain, for control of Lebanon and Syria. In the wake of the Free French victory, Beirut was gripped by years of political tension and turmoil as Lebanon demanded its independence.

Meanwhile, ACS remained open. The school leaders wisely ended the 1940-1941 school year early, thus avoiding potential casualties from the aerial bombardments of the British invasion. ACS then reopened in the fall of 1941. The ACS Board of Trustees turned to twenty-two year old Ivy Cleo Gorkiewicz, a dynamic young principal, for leadership. Gorkiewicz's vision was to make the school a more Lebanese institution.

The First Signs of War in Beirut

On September 3, 1939–two days after Nazi Germany invaded Poland–France and Britain declared war against Germany. Lebanon at the time was still under the French Mandate.

The American Community School was preparing to open for its thirty-fifth school year in September 1939. The parents of many ACS students had lived in Beirut through the First World War. The following account, written by a Lebanese teacher, captured the widespread feelings of fear:

> *In early September 1939 we were preparing for the new school year when the airwaves carried terror to our souls, pounding us all day with news reports of the Second World War. In the next few days, I saw acute pain rise in the breasts of the generation that had lived through the catastrophe of the First World War... Work stopped and a wave of pessimism engulfed the country.*[2]

As people put their lives on hold, ACS parents, students, and faculty were consumed by the news on the radio.

By January 1940, three months after the beginning of the war, over 100,000 French soldiers were stationed across Lebanon and Syria.[3] Thereafter, the troops arrived in Ras Beirut. The soldiers were mostly "colonials" from Senegal under the command of French officers. Their presence in front of AUB and along the Corniche came as a surprise to ACS students.[4] The war increasingly disrupted everyday life. As the Senegalese soldiers dug trenches on strategic hilltops and along the coast, government rationing began. Gasoline was scarce. One ACS parent, Bayard Dodge, put a positive face on gas rationing. "Since there isn't any gasoline, I'm getting my exercise by walking more," he wrote in a letter.[5] ACS students were not quite as positive about the rationing of sugar, however. The lack of sugar meant that favorites such as chocolate "muds," ambrosial confections consisting of vanilla ice cream topped with chocolate sauce, malted milk and whipped cream, were no longer available at the soda fountain opposite the main gate of AUB.[6]

Figure 4.2: ACS students, faculty, and staff in 1940. (Curtis Strong at the right of the third row from the back.)

The war posed more serious threats. A strict blackout was enforced including the painting of car headlights.[7] By the spring of 1940, residents anticipated German U-boat attacks in Beirut's harbor. The fear of starvation became more dangerous than the reality of starvation. Rumors of famine prompted bread marches that sometimes turned violent.[8]

Meanwhile, in Europe, France collapsed under the weight of the German blitz. By June 1940, France signed an armistice, and a puppet state of Vichy France became Hitler's official ally. Therefore, in the summer of 1940, Vichy-controlled Lebanon became an ally of the Axis powers.

Beirut under Vichy Control

When France fell, some ACS community members evacuated. Rhoda Orme, the school's principal for most of the 1930s, returned to the United States. Curtis Strong, a popular English and history teacher, replaced her as principal for the 1940-1941 school year although he had no administrative experience. He first coped with a trickle of student departures, which turned into a flood as the war made its way towards Beirut.

In the summer of 1940, Marshal Philippe Petain, the leader of Vichy France, sent his emissary, General Henri Dentz, to rule Beirut. German officials appeared in Beirut for the first time and helped train the local police force. German propaganda appeared in Lebanese newspapers.[9] Under Vichy rule, the cost of living in Beirut doubled. Taxis were banned to conserve gasoline, bread lines increased, and local political organizations such as the Phalange and Najjada began protesting in the streets.[10]

Military activity also intensified. Trenches continued to be dug. Instead of defending Beirut from an Axis attack, Senegalese troops prepared against the British and Free French forces attacking from Palestine in the south. Beirut now witnessed French soldiers fighting French soldiers.[11] The allied attack did not come until a year later, which gave the Vichy Army time to prepare and the civilians of Beirut plenty of time for anxiety. "The digging of large trenches, the continued blackouts at night, and the building of bomb shelters, made everyone realize that war was near at hand," recalled Bayard Dodge, the president of AUB.[12]

Throughout this period, Curtis Strong was charged with overseeing ACS. The Lebanese expected not only a British invasion from Palestine but also a German invasion from the northwest. By May 1941, Germany had conquered Greece and Crete. The planes of the German Air Force landed in Aleppo and several other Syrian airfields.[13] The mood within the communities of ACS and AUB was one of impending disaster. Meanwhile, Strong and Dodge waited for the right time to evacuate their students and teachers.[14]

May 1941: The Evacuation of ACS

By May 1941, ACS parents and Curtis Strong had been preparing for a school closure and evacuation for months.[15] The final decision to evacuate came on Monday, May 19.[16] On that morning, AUB President Dodge called a meeting with the leaders of the Protestant Mission and Strong to inform them about "secret intelligence" that he had received: Dodge's British contacts had revealed the plans of an imminent British assault on Beirut.[17]

After meeting with Dodge, Strong immediately called an assembly of the ACS faculty and students. He declared that "school was over for the year." According to Strong, "jubilation reigned" when the student body heard that summer was coming a month early. Students were then told to go directly home.[18]

Decades later, Curtis Strong recalled the efficiency and focus of the ACS faculty in this moment of crisis. Since the school year was over, final grades had to be calculated. Teachers took the time to write impromptu but personalized report cards for each student. Then they organized school supplies and closed the facility, all in expectation that ACS could reopen in the near, but unknown, future. ACS teachers accomplished this in less than two days. Strong led the operation, and thanks to his efforts, ACS did indeed open in the fall of 1941 with minimal disruption.[19] Strong, however, left in the evacuation and never returned to work at ACS.

ACS parents prepared for the evacuation with equal intensity and focus. One boy returned home after Strong's assembly to find his parents packing and a taxi waiting to take them to Jerusalem. Another said that his suitcases were packed even before Strong's announcement. Parents, many of whom were AUB faculty, had already planned many of the details of their evacuation. At least seven families – the Dodds, Kerrs, Leavitts, Ritschers, Smiths, Wests, Closes and Crawfords – crammed into taxis and headed south on May 20, arriving in Jerusalem that evening.

The ACS children in the caravan endured a memorable day. Some remembered their discomfort in the crammed, hot taxis. Some recalled their taxi breaking down and having to change cars. Others remembered the military checkpoints at Sidon, Tyre and the Palestinian border, where "sinister looking" Vichy French soldiers and "surly French officers" glared at the Americans on their way south. The Dodd family never forgot falling behind in the caravan and then being held up at gunpoint, "robbed by bandits." Their driver was shot in the jaw.[20] One student wrote decades later:

> As we drove through the tunnel at Ras Naqqura we saw a British Tommy silhouetted against the sky at the Palestinian end, his old-fashioned British helmet cocked at a rakish angle, standing at a stiff 'parade rest', with his old Lee-Enfield rifle thrust forward with a long bayonet on its end. He came to attention as we passed. My mother burst into tears.[21]

May 20, 1941 was perhaps the most hectic day of these parents' lives. The adults within the ACS community abruptly abandoned their homes in Beirut. For ACS children, it was mostly an adventure and an opportunity to miss school. For the parents, however, it was traumatic and one can easily understand the tears.

Bombs over Beirut

Most ACS families who fled to Palestine made their way back to the United States. Some families, however, remained in Beirut. These families contended with aerial bombings, invading armies, food shortages, and subsequent political turmoil. ACS was their refuge through it all.

Taxi Driver

All Deeb sees I see
purple iris   a mountain coat
of arms   goats cluttering

the road   stones clattering
the mudguards   every wolf
that used to be He lets me sit

in front beside the gear shift
for luck   blue camel beads
swinging from the rear view

mirror in which his mouth
is talking Arabic   We stop
at the sign of a Red Horse

flying   He pumps blue gas
dusts the dash and crested
hood   leaving time behind

- Allen West '48

The British and Free French invasion of Lebanon began on June 8, 1941.[22] Initially, a British cruiser attacked a Vichy French destroyer in the sea adjacent the AUB campus. The naval action was followed by 29 British air raids over Beirut. Shrapnel rained down on Ras Beirut and AUB's campus. Despite a sense of security, "the anti-aircraft barrage was deafening and large pieces of shells were liable to land anywhere in the city."[23] There is no record of the small ACS campus suffering any serious damage from the aerial bombings. However, one can assume that ACS was not exempt from the "shrapnel that scattered everywhere" over Ras Beirut, some of which was "unpleasantly large pieces" of burning lead, as the AUB president mildly put it.[24]

The battle did not last long in Lebanon. On June 15, the British captured Sidon on a quick march up the Lebanese coast. On June 22, Damascus fell to the British which coincidentally was the day that Germany launched Operation Barbarossa, Hitler's ultimately disastrous invasion of the Soviet Union. From that day on, it became clear to the Vichy French regime in Beirut that their German ally would not resupply them. Operation Barbarossa made the Soviet Union the focus of Hitler's war, and Germany effectively conceded Syria and Lebanon to the British.[25] On July 14, 1941, after firing a few rounds at the advancing British, the Vichy regime sued for peace.[26]

While the Free French replaced the Vichy forces, the real power in Syria and Lebanon was General Spears with the British Army backing him. Although the fighting in Beirut was over, instability continued. The Free French had fewer resources with which to feed the population, and the cost of food quickly rose 450 percent.[27] Hunger marches, led now by nationalist organizations, turned into demands for independence. Workers went on strike, diminishing the economic incentives for the French to maintain their mandate.[28] In 1943, when the French arrested Riad Al

Solh and Bechara El Khoury, the leaders of the Lebanese independence movement, Beirut was the scene of massive demonstrations.[29] That event prompted the president of AUB to write, "it looks as though the country might be plunged into an orgy of violence."[30] Violence was narrowly averted on November 22 when, after the intervention of General Spears, the French released the Lebanese leaders. This would ultimately lead to Lebanon's independence.

ACS reopened for the 1941-1942 school year. Despite the food shortage, the riots and the political upheavals, ACS remained open under the new leadership of Ivy Cleo de Gorkiewicz.

Gorkiewicz's Leadership

Ivy Gorkiewicz was born in Beirut in 1918, the child of a British mother and a Polish father. Her father arrived in 1914 to work for the Ottoman Water Company, and he remained in the city as a shipping manager.[31] Ivy attended her first classes at ACS in 1926 but initially she did not fit in with the mostly American expatriate students. She remembered being teased because of her Polish name.[32] Ivy persevered, however, and she graduated from ACS in 1935. After attending Exeter University in England, she returned to Beirut to teach in another English-speaking school prior to the 1941-1942 school year.

Figure 4.3: Ivy Cleo Gorkiewicz and Olga Holenkoff, 1943

The summer of 1941 was a chaotic time. The governing board of the school – a collection of parents, representatives of AUB and representatives of the Protestant Mission – were scattered across several continents. ACS trustee Mary Dodge, wife of the president of AUB, had returned to Beirut and asked Gorkiewicz to assume the burdens of leading ACS just a few weeks after the end of fighting in Beirut.[33] Gorkiewicz was certain that Mary Dodge chose her as principal because "I was familiar with all the traditions."[34]

Gorkiewicz received valuable assistance from Mary Dodge who played an important role in obtaining operating funds and recruiting faculty and students. Gorkiewicz also received support from Professor Julius Arthur Brown. Brown, the newly appointed dean of Faculty of the College of Arts and Sciences and a veteran of the AUB faculty, had taught physics and astronomy for over forty years.[35] He had remained at AUB through the famine and disease of World War I, and his insight and wisdom must have been invaluable to Gorkiewicz.[36] She thus had some of the most important and talented figures within the AUB community behind her.

ACS reopened in October 1941. The school had just 30 pupils – a decrease in enrollment of over 50 percent from the previous spring. Children of a few missionary families who had remained in Beirut returned to school.[37] But these were the exceptions. Gorkiewicz therefore filled her enrollment with as many "local people" as she could find.[38] Thus, ACS became more Lebanese in its student population.

As with the student body, the faculty became more diverse. Gorkiewicz recruited or retained five teachers: two returnees from the previous year and three new hires. Madame Holenkoff, the beloved Russian-born French language teacher, returned to her post, as did Kenneth Crose '34, an ACS graduate and humanities teacher. A Danish teacher, a Lebanese teacher, and an Armenian teacher completed the ranks of the faculty. ACS now had its first local teachers, Mr. Parounag Tovmassian and Ms. Malouf.

Figure 4.4: Mr. Tovmassian, one of the first local teachers hired by ACS.

Classes, which already were small before the war, became even smaller. Gorkiewicz's English literature class consisted of two pupils who met in her office.[39] As in the First World War, parents volunteered to fill the other teaching vacancies.[40] ACS's wartime students recalled that classes felt more like one-on-one tutorial sessions than traditional school.[41] Yet school leaders maintained a semblance of normalcy throughout the war. Madam Holenkoff, for example, continued to direct student dances and recitals. The school still hosted events like Parents' Day and the French picnic. The school continued to take field trips, sometimes ski days – when students used "old tin trays" as sleds.[42] Gorkiewicz also organized graduation each year in the school courtyard, even when there were only one or two graduates.[43]

In this environment, Gorkiewicz made a major change for which she was passionate. She hired a local Lebanese teacher to teach Arabic. During its first 36 years, ACS never offered the Arabic language as a class. It was an omission that several students found perplexing.[44] The young principal took advantage of the disruption of the war to make the necessary change. "I had always thought the non-teaching of Arabic a strange lacuna in the curriculum," Gorkiewicz explained years later.[45] Indeed, for years Gorkiewicz felt that failure to offer Arabic to children living in an Arabic-speaking country "was a terrible, terrible, oversight." The irony is that, despite growing up in Beirut, Gorkiewicz had never learned to read or write Arabic. Perhaps not having had the opportunity to learn the language led her to push so passionately to offer the subject to her students.[46]

The war impacted the lives of every member of the community. British and French soldiers were a daily presence in Ras Beirut – on the streets, in cafes and at movie theaters.[47] Gorkiewicz and the ACS community responded by avoiding the revolutionary movements altogether. Gorkiewicz did not remember World War II as a time of fear. "I was too busy running the school to worry about much else. Actually we had a lot of fun, because I was very young."[48]

Figure 4.5: Ms. Malouf

The Start of a Dual Identity

ACS, with the support and advice of the leaders of AUB, endured through the end of World War II. In the process, school enrollment was cut in half; new leadership was appointed; and new faculty replaced a dedicated group who had overseen the school's growth in the 1930s. The Board of Trustees reduced to three members who sacrificed their time and donated their efforts to assure that the school remained open.

The European war ended in the spring and summer of 1945. Ivy Cleo Gorkiewicz did not return to ACS as principal in the fall of 1945. "When the war was virtually over," Cleo wrote years later, "the governing board decided, very naturally, to re-employ American staff. It was suggested I should stay on as one of the teachers but I did not think this was a very good idea vis-à-vis the pupils." Instead of accepting a reduced role in the post-war ACS, Gorkiewicz "bade farewell to four very happy years" as the school's principal.[49] In the midst of wartime and her leadership of ACS, Gorkiewicz met, fell in love with, and married a British officer stationed in Beirut.[50] They eventually moved to England and had three sons.

Gorkiewicz's tenure as the school principal was a turning point in ACS's history. For 36 years, ACS had only hired American and European teachers. For 36 years, the student body was predominantly American. In the crisis of World War II, the school turned to Lebanese students and faculty for its survival. Since its inception, the school had focused on providing an American education. During World War II, school leaders adjusted that mission to offer Arabic. In the process, ACS became a more dynamic and less isolated place.

Thus began a trend that ultimately led to the school's 21st century dual-identity: both American and Lebanese, local and foreign, English-speaking and Arabic-speaking. As these changes were occurring, ACS underwent its greatest transformation to date. In the wake of World War II, representatives of a third sponsor, an oil company known as Aramco, the Arabian American Oil Company based in Saudi Arabia, joined representatives of AUB and the Protestant Mission on the school's Board of Trustees.

Notes

[1] Thompson [2000, p. 225]

[2] Thompson [2000, p. 225]

[3] Thompson [2000, p. 229]

[4] West [2010]

[5] Dodge [1941a]

[6] West [2010]

[7] West [2010]

[8] Kassir [2010, pp. 337-342]

[9] Dodge [1958, p. 71]

[10] Thompson [2000, p. 230]

[11] Kassir [2010, p. 342]

[12] Dodge [1958, p. 73]

[13] Dodge [1958, p. 72]

[14] Dodge [1941a]

[15] West [2010]

[16] West [2011a]

[17] Steward [1941]

[18] Stacey [1997, p. 32]

[19] Stacey [1997, pp. 31-32]

[20] West [2010]

[21] West [2010, Citing Raymond Close '47]

[22] Dodge [1958, p. 73]

[23] Dodge [1958, p. 74]

[24] Dodge [1941b]

[25] Dodge [1958, p. 75]

[26] Thompson [2000, p. 231]

[27] Thompson [2000, p. 231]

[28] Thompson [2000, p. 233]

[29] Kassir [2010, pp. 342-343]

[30] Dodge [1958, p. 86]

[31] Compton-Bishop [2012]

[32] Compton-Bishop [1996]

[33] Stacey [1997, p. 34]

[34] Compton-Bishop [1996]

[35] Dodge [1958, p. 28]

[36] Dodge [1958, p. 80]

[37] Dodge [1943]

[38] Compton-Bishop [1996]

[39] Compton-Bishop [1996]

[40] Compton-Bishop [1996]

[41] FitzHugh [2004]

[42] Compton-Bishop [1996]

[43] Stacey [1997, pp. 34-35]

[44] Bliss [2003, pp. 224-225]; Seelye [2004]

[45] Stacey [1997, p. 33]

[46] Compton-Bishop [1996]

[47] Dodge [1958, p. 82]

[48] Compton-Bishop [1996]

[49] Stacey [1997, p. 35]

[50] Compton-Bishop [1996]

5 Aramco and Expansion, 1946-1959

Figure 5.1: ACS's new campus

For both ACS and the city of Beirut, the decade and a half after World War II was an era of growth. Ras Beirut, once a collection of gardens and mulberry plantations, became filled with hotels, pubs, cafés, and movie theaters. In the 1950s, the Mayflower Hotel in the Hamra area and the Riviera Hotel along the Corniche were constructed. Anglophone bars such as Your Father's Moustache, Mr. Pickwick, the Rose & Crown, and the Duke of Wellington replaced what had been empty lots and pastoral landscape.[1] Inside these establishments, jazz and American pop songs filled the air instead of traditional Arabic tunes. American cocktails replaced arak.[2] Hamra Street was transformed from a dusty, red-clay road to a center of consumerism and café culture. Meanwhile, ACS once again remade itself.

The Immediate Aftermath of World War II

When Richard Ford became principal in the fall of 1945, there were just a few dozen pupils at ACS. The staff consisted of a handful of local and American teachers, two of whom were holdovers from the pre-war ACS. By 1947, at the end of Ford's second year as principal, the enrollment of the school had more than tripled to 92. Ford converted the top two floors of the schoolhouse, formerly used for the Boarding Department, into classrooms and found a second building a few blocks away to rent for boarders. [3]

Figure 5.2: One of the last groups to board on Rue Sidani, 1948

The post-war growth from 1945 through 1949 was at times unsettling for students, parents, and teachers. Of the 25 pupils in the high school in 1947, only nine had been in attendance the previous year.[4] Not surprisingly, the winner of ACS's student council election campaigned on the promise of providing better orientation for new students.[5] Growth and change created frustrations with the school. New ACS parents attempted to circumvent Ford by complaining to the Board about the academic workload and unfair grading. Other parents objected to the allegedly rude behavior of the new students and argued that the newcomers were hurting the learning environment. [6] Teachers also struggled with the changes in school culture and complained about disrespectful behavior, crude music, and teenage girls wearing red lipstick and skirts above the ankles.[7]

With great energy, Richard Ford managed the growth and tension. He seemed to be everywhere doing everything within the school community. Ford taught Latin and math, sponsored the leather-working club, and supervised the Boarding Department where he also resided.[8] He was a strict disciplinarian who quickly suspended the off-campus privileges of boarders who misbehaved. Yet Ford could also be quite humane with his pupils.[9] One incident in 1950 demonstrated his wisdom and understanding of adolescence. That year, a young new teacher died after just a month at ACS. During an emergency assembly in which Ford announced the tragedy, a group of older boys laughed. That evening in the Boarding Department he asked the boys to meet with him in the second floor lounge. Instead of berating the young men, Ford explained to the boys, "When young people hear unexpected news like that they hardly know whether to cry or laugh. This is called hysterical laughter, and it's a perfectly normal reaction."[10] Bill Tracy '53 was one of those boys, and he never forgot it. Instead of making the teenagers feel guilty and ashamed, Ford showed wisdom and compassion.

Figure 5.3: Ford and faculty organizing field day, late 1940s

Aramco and a New Campus

In the fall of 1947, Thomas Ball '49 arrived in Beirut on his 17th birthday. He had spent the previous year, his sophomore year of high school, in California. His father had been reassigned to the newly formed Tapline, an American oil firm contracted to build an oil pipeline (the Trans-Arabian Pipeline) from Saudi Arabia to the Mediterranean coast in Lebanon. Ball, Gerry Gossens '51 and Marilyn Haskell '49 were at the vanguard of a new type of ACS student: the "oil kid." Ball and his mother tried to fit in with the families who had lived in Beirut for generations – the children of AUB professors and Christian missionaries – but it was the Ball family and others like them who would forever change ACS.[11]

"The taxi scene was almost the same as it is today, including the services where shared rides were possible and the fare from Ras Beirut to the Bourg was 25 piasters or *Al bourg bi rubah* (a quarter). Taxis also served ACS boys well too. One could rent a taxi (usually from a stand across from the AUB main gate) for ten pounds an hour and the cabdriver would teach us how to drive on the Corniche, a place underutilized compared to today! The instructions were in French with the appropriate Arabic accent such as *drob frem* (brake) *daas benzine* (accelerate), the *guidon* (steering wheel) and *wlah! hut debrayage* (use the clutch, boy!) There were Arabic lessons for the newly arrived American boys such as *yallah masheena* (let's go) *wa'if* (stop) and then the usual curse words when we messed up. The drivers liked the money but they seemed to enjoy their roles as teachers. We also learned the many words for a car: *autumbeel, makana, arabeeya, sayarah ...*"

- Sam Constan '53

The initiatives of the Ball, Gossens, and Haskell families to find a school for their children grew into an official sponsorship. Aramco, Tapline's parent company, headquartered in Saudi Arabia, needed a secondary school outside the Arabian Peninsula for the older children of their employees. According to Aramco, there were "social and academic problems related to the creation of American high schools in Saudi Arabia."[12] Apparently, the Saudi government requested that American children seek their secondary schooling elsewhere. Based on the positive reviews of families such as the Balls, Aramco made an offer to the ACS Board sometime during the 1947-1948 school year. The proposition: Aramco/Tapline would become a third sponsor of the school and would receive a guaranteed number of admission slots for its employees' children. In return, the oil company would fund the construction of a new campus with one building specifically designed to house and feed boarding students.[13]

This was one of the most important moments in the history of the school. Had the Board of Trustees wished to maintain the status quo at ACS, it could have easily turned down Aramco's offer. Indeed, the Board consisted of "old-guard" AUB families. William A. West '12, son of one of the three founders of the Faculty School, was on the Board, as was William Chandler.[14] Howard B. Leavitt '39, the grandson of AUB's founder, also took part in the decision. These men, all descendants of the Faculty School's founders, agreed to give up some of their control in favor of expansion.

Figure 5.4: The Trans-Arabian Pipeline carried crude oil from Aramco's fields in Saudi Arabia to the shipping terminal at Zahrani south of Sidon, 1950

In 1948, the ACS families took on the project of a new campus with enthusiasm. The Board chose two parcels of land down the hill from the existing school off Rue Jeanne d'Arc and just below the International College campus. A long set of stairs that ran from Bliss Street down to the new campus was dubbed the "prep stairs." The two new school buildings were completed quickly, although not soon enough for the start of school in October 1949. Workers were still putting the finishing touches on the high school building as classes resumed for the year. The Boarding Department would not be completed until the fall of 1950, so boarders lived up the hill in the old campus for a final year. They walked up and down "the prep stairs" several times a day. The entire community rallied together in the final days of construction. Parents helped move books into the library and carried desks down from the old campus.[15] Teachers cleaned their classrooms as construction continued in the hallways.[16] This was made more difficult because the steps at the front were unfinished on opening day, causing awkward foot traffic that spread mud on the new floors.[17]

Figure 5.5: The Boarding Department building, also known as the "BD", completed in 1950

From 1945 through 1949, growth and transition became a part of ACS's identity. Richard Ford wrote in 1949 that "We are forever on the move; our school is always in a state of flux."[18]. The leaders of ACS in the 1920s and 1930s would not have used those words to describe their school, nor would they describe their student body as "globe-trotters" as Ford did in 1949. Prior to World War II, ACS had served families who had established permanent residency in Beirut and the surrounding areas. Now, ACS was increasingly a transient place where students arrived and departed with their parents' Aramco or State Department postings. "We enjoyed our new classrooms," one teacher recalled, "but somehow... I felt a queasy sadness in my stomach that the old ACS, the 'real' ACS, was about to disappear forever."[19]

The 1950s Student Body: More American and More Oil Kids

The most obvious change to ACS in the early 1950s, aside from the new campus, was the number of students enrolled. In 1947, ACS had fewer than 100 students.[20] In 1949 the number increased to 149, by 1953 there were 355 students, and by 1957 there were 437.[21] In 1949, Aramco/Tapline students, the "oil kids," represented 16 percent of ACS's student body.[22] By 1953, oil kids made up 42 percent of the student body.[23] Fewer and fewer of ACS's students considered Beirut their permanent home. Only two of the graduating 26 seniors in the class of 1954 were born and raised in Beirut.[24] Increasingly, students had closer ties to the United States and weaker ties to Lebanon.

Figure 5.6: Students in the 1950s put the new library to good use

The new students also brought regional identities from the United States. For these students, "home" was a specific town and state in America. Members of the class of 1959 claimed Texas, New York, Ohio, California, Minnesota, Wyoming, and Colorado as their homes.[25] Playful regional rivalries emerged. Ruthie Ellen Renfer '52 identified herself as the "little girl from Texas;" Dave Engen '54 listed his greatest pet peeve as "states other than Montana;" and Mary Thweatt '55 wanted to make Texas a republic again.[26] John A. Fitzgerald '54, from Virginia, was called a "rebel through and through" by his classmates while Galan Leeman '55 complained that he was tired of "Bragging Texans."[27]

In the 1950s, it was the school's official policy to keep ACS as American as possible.[28] To ensure that space was available for the children of American citizens, the Board required special approval for the admittance of all "non-American" children. In 1954, for instance, the Board gave approval for the admission of five German, eight Chinese, three Dutch, five British, and two Colombian students, but only because "the cases are too few to create a problem of space for American applicants."[29] In an August 1955 meeting, the Board passed a resolution "to emphasize that we do everything to encourage Middle Eastern and especially Lebanese students to make use of the Lebanese schools."[30] In effect, Lebanese students were discouraged from applying. In 1955, only ten percent of the total student body, or between 30 and 40 students, were not Americans.[31] Included in those several dozen students were Iranian children like Nasrin Malayeri '60, Armenians like Pakrad Kazazian '55, and several Chinese students like Shino-Ling.[32] These students, however, were the exception to the explicit rule that ACS was for Americans in the 1950s.[33]

Figure 5.7: The ACS Corniche campus in the late 1950s

The New Faculty: Young, American, and Transient

In addition to building a new campus, Aramco also promised funds for the recruitment and retention of the "best American faculty." Richard Ford, the principal, was responsible for hiring these new teachers, and he had only two weeks each spring to travel to the U.S., contact, interview and hire new teachers.[34] This was a challenging task. Administrators therefore tended to rely on younger, less experienced teachers willing to serve overseas. These young teachers were hired directly upon their graduations from universities and colleges such as Dartmouth, St. Lawrence, Oberlin, and Harvard's School of Education. In 1957, ACS hired six new teachers with only one or two years of experience and four new teachers with no experience at all.[35] Some of these young teachers were excellent. Many students from the 1950s remembered that their favorite teachers were young, dynamic, and at times lacking in experience.[36] What they lacked in experience, the young teachers made up for with enthusiasm and dedication.[37]

The faculty in the 1950s built meaningful relationships with their students who never forgot them. Mrs. Kadi was a 26-year-old English teacher who was "fantastic," but also "kind of a hippie," as one student put it.[38] Mrs. Albright, a history teacher, was known for her warmth and sense of humor.[39] Mr. Royal, called the "crazy Americanized Englishman," assumed the role of English teacher, drama director, and dean of Boys.[40] George Zarour taught physics and chemistry and was described as "an incredible teacher."[41] The 1958 yearbook was dedicated to Zarour. It cited his "unfailing sense of humor and consideration for the individual inside and out of the classroom."[42] Ms. Parnell was a young and dynamic biology teacher who also served as the dean of Girls. Students remembered Parnell's Tennessee charm and southern drawl.[43] However, as with so many young and talented teachers, Parnell left Beirut after just a few years.

On the other hand, Wilfred and Elsa Turmelle stayed for over thirty years. Wilfred Turmelle arrived in 1951 as a middle school social studies teacher. Students instantly loved him, calling him "Uncle Willie."[44] There was an interesting quirk to Wilfred: his glass eye. Wilfred would take the eye out of its socket and place it on his desk as he left the classroom, reminding students, "I'm watching you." In one prank, two students took Wilfred's spare glass eye and put it in a classmate's drink. Wilfred laughed off the prank.[45] Elsa Jane Putnam arrived in 1954, three years after her soon-to-be husband, Wilfred Turmelle. From the students' perspective, Wilfred and Elsa were destined to be together.[46]

Figure 5.8: George Zarour, one of the most popular teachers
at ACS for over a decade

During their courtship, Elsa taught physical education, created the Girls
Athletic Association, organized a pep squad to promote school spirit,
and was eventually promoted to dean of girls.[47] In their thirty years
at the school, they were more than teachers and administrators. They
were mother and father figures to generations of ACS students.[48]

Life in the Boarding Department: "I Couldn't Stand the Fascism."

As a boarding school, ACS was responsible for the safety of its students.
For the administration, this translated into accountability, and the
school attempted to regulate nearly every aspect of student life. Bubble
gum and comic books were forbidden. Use of candy was discouraged.[49]
Portable radios were banned from dorm rooms.[50] "Lights out" occurred
promptly at 9:30 p.m. each weeknight. At 7:40 a.m. on weekdays rooms
were checked to assure tidiness.[51] Leaving campus was carefully mon-

Figure 5.9: The annual Sadie Hawkins dance

itored. If students sought leave from the campus, they were required to sign out in groups of four or more during the day and groups of six or more at night. If they wished to venture downtown, they were required to be accompanied by an adult chaperone.[52] Girls had to be accompanied by male escorts at all times.[53]

Some boarders rebelled against such restrictions. As one student reflected years later, "I couldn't stand the fascism."[54] The rebellion and mischief could be benign at times: Short sheeting a fellow student's bed, flying toy airplanes inside the boarding hallways, electrocuting a classmate's pet fish, or dumping water on people peering up an empty elevator shaft.[55] At other times, the infractions were quite serious. Some boys made rope ladders to visit one another's rooms at night, risking serious injury.[56] Periodically, students were caught drinking on campus. But, more frequently, boys would escape campus through dorm windows, drink off campus, and attempt to return undetected.[57]

By the mid-1950s, the boarders had developed reputations for lawlessness. The principal's efforts to "campus" boarders, or deny their off-campus privileges, proved ineffective. The Board of Trustees requested that Beirut parents not serve students alcohol off campus. But this did not stop the drinking.[58] The Board complained of a "general letdown in orderliness", and it formed a special committee to investigate "the shouts, the screams, the pushing and shoving in the halls, shorts and slacks and pin curls worn in class, and lack of manners in general."[59]

Ultimately, the Board held the principal responsible for the breakdown of behavior.

A Change of Leadership

Robert Bassett became principal of ACS in 1952. In addition to his duties as principal, Bassett taught philosophy, and he gave weekly chapel talks with titles such as "Keep Trying," "Broaden Your Interests," and "There's Always a Second Chance."[60] Students described Bassett as quiet and unassuming, but he also had a reputation as being determined and uncompromising.[61] Bassett oversaw the construction of a new wing of the Boarding Department, dealt with lawsuits over land claims, raised money for student financial aid, and began a campaign to build a new gym.[62] There were successes, but apparently the size and complexity of the school posed managerial challenges for a principal accustomed to smaller school operations. The Board voted seven to one to not renew Bassett's contract in 1956. The Board chair wrote a recommendation for Bassett explaining that he would be an effective administrator for smaller schools.[63]

Figure 5.10: Robert Bassett, 1954 and Clarence Schultz, 1957

The Board hired Dr. Clarence Schultz to replace Bassett.[64] Schultz seemed to fit the role of a prep school principal. He wore tweed jackets and bow ties. He smoked a pipe. He exuded energy, confidence and enthusiasm, and he ran ACS accordingly. He held his teachers to higher standards with, for example, mandatory workshops on dorm parenting and a more formal coordination in the curriculum.[65] Schultz was also willing to fire teachers midyear, which he did after his first semester at ACS. As with teachers, Schultz held students accountable. In the first week of the 1956-1957 school year, Schultz suspended two boys for misbehavior. A few months later, he expelled another student for "having a bad influence in the school."[66] Meanwhile, he built stronger relationships with the parents, and he periodically traveled to Saudi Arabia to meet with Aramco parents.[67]

The responsibilities of the principal became greater than one person could handle. The Board hired a business manager, and Schultz received the additional support of an assistant principal.[68] The principal was increasingly becoming a fundraiser, especially after the Board launched a six-year campaign to fund the construction of a gymnasium. The goal was to raise $25,000. Aramco pledged $8,000.[69] Fundraising banquets were held each year in which students performed and provided food services. Monthly letters requested donations from parents. Even the fourth graders contributed by selling cakes.[70] By the end of Schultz's first year, 40 percent of parents had participated in a drive that raised $16,000 of the gym fund.[71] However, when the gym opened in the fall of 1958, Schultz was no longer leading ACS. A civil conflict within Lebanon had led to the exodus of teachers, administrators, and students and, ultimately, threatened ACS's existence.

The 1958 Crisis

The school community was not prepared for the conflict that broke out in May 1958. Earlier that spring, Schultz had returned from a successful faculty recruiting trip in the United States. He reported that American teachers were increasingly excited about the prospects of living and working in Beirut.[72] Thirty-two American families from across the Middle East had made inquiries about sending their children to ACS.[73] When the conflict began, the gunfire remained largely outside of Ras Beirut, although some ACS students recalled hearing the sound of machine gunfire at night.[74] As journalist and historian Samir Kassir put it, the violence, while claiming the lives of several hundred Lebanese, "had more of the quality of a murderous family quarrel than of a battle to the last bullet."[75]

Then on Friday, May 23, Schultz received a letter handwritten in Arabic. The letter contained a threat to bomb the school. It was signed "The Opposition," the title of one of the two warring factions within Lebanon. Schultz immediately contacted the police, the ACS Board, and parents. He also contacted Saeb Salam, a former Prime Minister and one of the principal leaders of the Opposition. Salam responded with assurances that no one in his organization had sent the letter. The police were

Figure 5.11: The ACS Board of Trustees meet with Schultz the year of the evacuation (Clarence Schultz at left and William Chandler pointing)

skeptical of the authenticity of the threat, and they concluded that, based on the handwriting, the letter was probably of a non-Arabic origin, perhaps from an American teenager pretending to be an Arab. Thus, the authorities believed that the incident was a prank by ACS students.[76]

However, in the three weeks prior to the letter, a bomb had exploded in Souk Tawile, another bomb had been found on a tram downtown, and a third bomb had been placed at a local Jewish school. A representative of the U.S. Embassy visited ACS and advised an early end to the school year. Schultz and his Board agreed with the Embassy's recommendation.[77] With only fifteen days remaining in the school year, ACS closed for the summer. Boarding students were evacuated within a week.[78]

Schultz then resigned as principal, which left the school leaderless for several months.[79] Almost a third of the faculty also resigned and the Board faced the distinct possibility that its students would not return. After the evacuation, the Board was able to contact only 90 of the 400 students scattered across Cyprus, Greece, Italy, and the United States.[80] Then on June 12, Aramco withdrew its sponsorship of ACS. It was an "action which may have a devastating effect upon the school," the Board recorded. "Premature and unwarranted," one Board member added. "Should ACS be unable to open this fall, parents of hundreds of students from Beirut and other points in the Middle East will be forced to make other schooling arrangements," the Board protested.[81] By mid-July, ACS teetered on the edge of permanent closure.

The seven members of the Board, led by its president William Chandler, believed that most of the students would return. The Board met every two weeks that summer and planned for an enrollment of 350 students in the ensuing school year. All teachers were encouraged to return and the Boarding Department would remain open. Numerous letters went to American families stating that ACS would go about its business in the 1958-1959 school year. The Board did delay the opening day of school for two weeks. Most importantly, ACS changed its admissions policies. The Board stated that academic standards would not be lowered, but it reversed the American-centered policy by stating that "non-American children, with adequate command of English, could be given more encouragement [to apply]."[82] Once again, in a moment of crisis, the American Community School willingly became less American.

Interestingly, that summer ACS hosted the United States Marine Corps. As the Board scrambled to save the school, Lebanon's President Camille Chamoun called on his ally, the United States, to intervene in the civil conflict. On July 15, several thousand Marines landed in Beirut.[83] Those Marines needed places to sleep and the U.S. Embassy requested the use of ACS's campus as barracks for a handful of the Marines. The Board agreed, and for two months the Boarding Department and high-school buildings became a home of the United States Marine Corps. Upon departure, the Marines left behind several thousand dollars' worth of damage and missing items, for which the ACS Board filed a lawsuit to recover.[84]

After a chaotic summer that witnessed an evacuation, Aramco's abandonment, a vacuum of leadership and the Marine occupation, ACS reopened on October 15, 1958. Only 138 students attended the first day of classes. The Board met the next day to discuss its options. Although the conditions did not merit optimism, the Board held wisdom and experience. Curtis Strong, the former principal of ACS during the early days of World War II, was a member of the governing seven. So was Mary Dale Dorman. The wife of Harry Dorman, she had fled Beirut in 1941 to the Western Hemisphere to avoid German submarines.[85] These people had lived through conflict in the Middle East. They kept calm. Gradually, students began to return. By November, enrollment had increased to 258. By January, 335 students were attending the school which was near full capacity. Aramco then reinstituted its sponsorship of ACS. The Board's gamble had paid off.

A student graduating from ACS in 1948 would not have recognized the school of a decade later. ACS had built a new campus in a new location. Enrollment had quadrupled. The composition of the student body was no longer just the children of AUB professors and missionaries. Unlike the "old guard" families of ACS, the new "oil kids" were more familiar with Houston, Southern California, and Colorado than Beirut. As a result, the school experienced growing pains, management problems, and discipline issues. However, for the predominantly American student body of the era, the school "felt" American, and it served well the academic and social needs of that student population. The records reflect that the Americans who were students at ACS in the 1950s overwhelmingly were grateful to the school for their education and experiences there.

Then the conflict of 1958 threatened a decade of growth. The Board, comprised of a dedicated group of ACS graduates and parents, rallied to support the school. To compensate for the sudden decline in enrollment and for the second time in two decades, ACS opened its doors to Lebanese children. But when prosperity returned, and when the conflict subsided, ACS again restricted the admission of children who were not Americans.

Notes

[1] Kassir [2010, p. 396]

[2] Kassir [2010, pp. 389-390]

[3] ACS [d, 1956], Stacey [1997, p. 45]

[4] The Record, "Next Year? An Improvement?" May28, 1947

[5] The Record, "Student Council Elections" May 28, 1947

[6] West [2011c]

[7] Compton-Bishop [1996]

[8] Stacey [1997, p. 38]; ACS [d, 1949]; Tracy [2004, 2004]

[9] West [2011c]

[10] Tracy [2004]

[11] Stacey [1997, pp. 36-37]

[12] Chandler [1963]

[13] Chandler [1963]

[14] William Chandler was also one of Tapline's earliest employees. [Editor's note]

[15] West [2011b]

[16] Shamma [2005]

[17] West [2011b]

[18] ACS [d, 1949]

[19] Stacey [1997, p. 46]

[20] West [2011b]

[21] ACS Board of Trustees, September 25, 1957

[22] West [2011b]

[23] ACS Board of Trustees, February 15, 1955

24 *ACS [d, 1954]*

25 *ACS [d, 1954]*

26 ACS [d, 1951]; ACS [d, 1953]

27 ACS [d, 1954]; ACS [d, 1955]

28 ACS Board of Trustees, 1955

29 ACS Board of Trustees, July 19, 1954

30 ACS Board of Trustees, August 4, 1955

31 ACS Board of Trustees, September 27, 1955

32 ACS Board of Trustees, September 14, 1954; Tracy [2004]; ACS Board of Trustees, March 15, 1955; ACS [e, June 7, 1954]

33 ACS Board of Trustees, November 1, 1955

34 ACS Board of Trustees, August 4, 1955

35 ACS Board of Trustees, May 27, 1957

36 McFeaters [2005]

37 Tracy [2004]; Stacey [2005]

38 Miller [2004]; Samuel [2004]

39 ACS [d, 1956]; Tracy [2004]

40 ACS [d, 1955]

41 Miller [2004]

42 ACS [d, 1958]

43 ACS [d, 1954]

44 Stacey [2005]

45 Tracy [2004]

46 Stacey [1997, p. 56]

47 ACS Board of Trustees, June 10, 1957

48 Stacey [1997, p. 56]

49 ACS [a, 1951]

50 Miller [2004]

51 ACS [a, 1955-1956]

52 Stacey [2005]

53 Samuel [2004]

54 Lund [2004]

55 Tracy [2004]; Stacey [1997, p. 40]; ACS [d, 1951]

56 ACS [e, April 29, 1955]

57 Miller [2004]; Stacey [1997, p. 44]

58 ACS Board of Trustees, January 13, 1953

59 ACS Board of Trustees, Confidential supplement: December 13, 1955

60 ACS [e, November 1953]

61 ACS [d, 1953]; ACS Board of Trustees, Confidential supplement: December 8, 1955

62 ACS Board of Trustees, April 21, 1953; May 26, 1953; November 17, 1953; February 9, 1954; November 2, 1953

63 ACS Board of Trustees, January 3, 1956

64 ACS Board of Trustees, January 16, 1956

65 ACS Board of Trustees, September 17, 195

66 ACS Board of Trustees, January 25, 1957; February 25, 1957

67 ACS [d, 1958]

68 ACS Board of Trustees, June 26, 1957

69 ACS Board of Trustees, August 22, 1957

70 ACS [f, February 21, 1955; No date given]

71 ACS [f, April 22, 1957]

72 ACS Board of Trustees, March 27, 1958

73 ACS Board of Trustees, April 17, 1958

74 Kassir [2010, p. 455]

75 Kassir [2010, p. 455]

76 ACS Board of Trustees, Special Meeting, May 23, 1958

77 ACS Board of Trustees, Special Meeting, May 23, 1958

78 ACS Board of Trustees, May 29, 1958

79 ACS Board of Trustees, June 26, 1958

80 ACS Board of Trustees, August 1, 1958

81 ACS Board of Trustees, June 12, 1958

82 ACS Board of Trustees, August 26, 1958

83 Crawford [1972b, p. 41]

84 ACS Board of Trustees, October 3, 1958

85 ACS Board of Trustees, October 16, 1958

6 The "Golden American Ghetto," 1959-1967

Figure 6.1: The recently completed gymnasium in 1959

Catherine Bashshur and Laila Faris Alamuddin '62, two pillars of the ACS community, used the same phrase to describe ACS in the 1960s: "American ghetto."[1] Bashshur arrived in the fall of 1964 as a middle school social studies teacher. Alamuddin graduated from ACS in 1962 and held many roles over the years including director of college guidance, dean of students, assistant principal and acting principal. As Bashshur and Alamuddin explained, the school community in the 1960s strove to recreate the culture and comforts of the United States. In doing this, ACS reinforced its isolation from its Beirut community. Thus, as they explained, it had become an "American ghetto." A 1964 questionnaire to ACS parents phrased it slightly differently. The questionnaire asked parents to explain whether or not they thought the school formed a "golden ghetto."[2] The decade after the 1958 crisis saw the height of the American Community School's isolation – the period when ACS was "most American." Yearbooks, student newspapers, school brochures, Board meeting minutes and chapel talks all reinforced this American characteristic. However, teachers, students and trustees were concerned about the school's isolation during the 1960s, and some steps were taken to expose students to the broader community of Beirut. Thus, ACS in the 1960s was a paradox: it desired to "feel American" while at the same time it recognized the importance of allowing its students to experience the culture and society in which they lived.

Figure 6.2: Mia Knox, Rita Knox, Darcy Knox, Dwight Knox, Charlotte Rahaim, and Jane Monroe, in September 1966. Dr. Dwight Knox was the first ACS leader designated "Headmaster".

ACS's Continued Growth

Despite the crises of 1958, ACS grew and matured in the late 1950s and early 1960s. The growth especially came in the form of new buildings and increased enrollment. The gymnasium and high-school auditorium were completed in the years after the 1958 evacuation. A new lower school was finally completed in 1961 and would be the last new

Figure 6.3: The new elementary school building in 1962

building at ACS for decades.[3] The new facilities were paid through "expansion fees" and Tapline's continued support. Aramco/Tapline, which had temporarily withdrawn its sponsorship in the summer of 1958, reengaged with the school that fall and contributed 100,000 Lebanese pounds (then roughly $45,000) to the capital campaign.[4]

In the 1960s, ACS developed into a complex institution with multiple layers of administration serving over 1,000 students. In 1959, 457 students attended ACS. By 1969, that number had increased to 1,010.[5] In 1959, the Board hired its first "Headmaster," Dr. Dwight Knox. In 1959, ACS also appointed lower-school, middle-school and high-school principals who oversaw each division. Sixty years after its creation, ACS had evolved from its beginnings as a family-run Faculty School into an institution which bore structural and governing similarities to the major private schools in the U.S.

Academics, Athletics and Christianity: Recreating Home at ACS

The composition of the study body was the principal reason ACS was described as an "American ghetto." Catherine Bashshur estimated that the student body was 90 percent American in the 1960s.[6] A student

66

who graduated in 1971 put the figure at 95 percent.[7] In reality, the percentages were lower. In 1969, 82 percent of the students at ACS were U.S. citizens. Remarkably, the remaining 18 percent represented 35 different nationalities.[8] Few of the non-Americans were Lebanese. Of the 94 non-American students in the late 1960s, only two were from Arab nations: one Egyptian and one Saudi. By 1970, there were no "fully" Lebanese students, meaning there were no students at ACS with only a Lebanese passport.[9]

ACS had always promised to prepare its students academically for American colleges. By the 1960s that promise was a reality. The school now had the teachers and the resources to recreate a truly American-style education.[10] In the 12th grade students were required to study American history. In middle school, the focus was on civics and U.S. government.[11] These came at the expense of non-Western history and culture. For example, the curriculum did not include Middle Eastern history.[12] Teachers sought to instill critical, independent thinking in their students, or the "development of free, creative thinking" as the 1961 yearbook described it.[13] Students were asked to memorize less and analyze more. They were encouraged to disagree with their teachers and to support their positions with facts. Such skills were necessary for a free, democratic society.[14]

Figure 6.4: The 1964 cheerleading squad, (left to right) Lynne Tietjen '65, Chris Call '65, Pat Deines '65, Lynn Davis '64 , Cleo Fagerlie '65, Nancy Burdick '66, Judy McKinley '64.

However, students complained about their workloads. Term papers were too time-consuming. Teachers, they believed, conspired to assign tests on the same day, especially at the end of a semester. Students believed that they had to sacrifice their social lives to academics.[15] In 1959, several Student Council members filed a formal complaint to the Board about the workload.[16] In 1968, parents requested a meeting with Board members about "academic pressure." They explained that their children "stay up late hours and drop other worthwhile activities such as private music lessons to meet academic demands."[17] Irrespective of the complaints, ACS delivered on its commitment to prepare teenagers for American universities. Eighty two percent of the class of 1969 went on to attend colleges and universities in the United States. Few, it seems, complained that they were academically unprepared.

Figure 6.5: Vespers Committee, in charge of organizing chapel, posing with Lebanese law enforcement on the Corniche, 1965

As with academics, the athletic programs of ACS were purposefully modeled on American sports. Baseball and football, in particular, allowed the boys to maintain their American athletic identities – despite the fact that they were thousands of miles away from home in a region that had little interest in those sports.[18] "The great American game [baseball] claims a high priority at ACS as it does wherever American boys are gathered," explained a school brochure beneath a picture of a boy swinging a bat.[19] However, there was little competition available in Lebanon for the school's baseball and football teams. The athletics department had to be creative. In addition to competing with local schools in soccer and basketball, a tradition developed where each grade formed a flag football team to compete with the other grades in a Thanksgiving tournament.[20] An entire baseball season might consist of six games. The 1967 team ended the year 1-6. These included understandable losses to teams representing AUB, the ACS faculty, and the U.S. Embassy.[21] Similarly, the girls' basketball and volleyball seasons were limited to three or four games a year, enhanced by ACS-only tournaments.[22]

Figure 6.6: American football in 1967 and ACSers at the popular AUB softball field in 1964

The school's mission of emphasizing Protestant Christianity also enhanced its American orientation despite the growing cynicism of the students. Religion was integral in the school's founding. However, by the 1960s, missionary families represented a small portion of the student population. The school now included "oil kids," some of whom were not Protestant or were more secular minded. Many boarders who signed out on Sundays to attend churches in Ras Beirut would instead go to the movies.[23] The school continued its tradition of prayers before meals, which had begun with the founding of the Boarding Department in 1921. Yet many of the boarders in the 1960s felt uncomfortable with the practice. Some refused to say grace and others recited sarcastic blessings in attempts at humor.[24]

Nonetheless, school leaders maintained Protestant traditions so familiar to America. A brochure in 1963 explained to prospective parents that "[ACS] has always been a Christian school, believing that the instruction and influences it provides must be consonant with the Christian philosophy."[25] In the 1960s, the school hired its first chaplain who taught religion and organized the weekly chapel services.[26] The Board Chair reassured parents that the school would always have a solid foundation in Christian values.[27] The operating assumption in the 1960s, while not necessarily true, was that every child was a Christian.[28] Speakers at weekly chapel services were principally from AUB, the Protestant Mission in Beirut, and various evangelical churches in Lebanon and Syria. These were, for the most part, Americans preaching to Americans.

Figure 6.7: The 1963 Girls Basketball team

Unintended Consequences

The school's curriculum and philosophy conveyed a subtle message to its students: Beirut outside of ACS is unsafe and untrustworthy. In fairness, ACS officials did have the obligation to protect boarders as the school acted in *loco parentis*, or in place of parents. However, the

Figure 6.8: The infamous "AUB stairs" stretched from the IC gate down to ACS

unintended consequence was to further isolate the American students in the "American ghetto."

ACS discouraged unregulated interaction with Lebanese teenagers.[29] "Girls must not appear on the streets in shorts," a 1961 newsletter decreed. Boys were instructed to avoid talking to local girls whom they did not know, and they expressly were told not to engage in arguments with local teenagers.[30] Other than occasional basketball games, relations with International College (IC), the neighboring school which had a more local student body, were distant. Nonetheless, students recalled engaging in "firecracker wars" with rival students by lobbing bottle rockets over school walls in what probably started as a good-natured prank.[31] Few students from the 1960s described having friends at neighboring IC.

Several incidents in the 1950s and 1960s supported the notion that ACS's students required protection from outsiders. There were reports of attacks on ACS girls in 1953.[32] In 1957, the Board hired a security officer to patrol the stairs from Bliss Street down to ACS. The officer apprehended a "molester" (a neighborhood boy) and handed him over to the police.[33] In 1963, an attacker ripped a girl's dress on the stairs. Later that year, a "prowler" broke into the girls' dorm, and a man was caught exposing himself in front of the playground. The final incident involved a group of Lebanese men who repeatedly drove by ACS in two Volkswagens "shouting dirty language from the cars at our teenagers."[34] The Board placed more restrictions on off-campus privileges and enlisted the help of the U.S. ambassador. As a result, by the end of 1963 the school was receiving around-the-clock police protection.[35]

Years later, ACS alumni remember the social isolation that resulted from tighter security and fear of harassment. "I think that they isolated us too much from Lebanon," JoAnn Atwood '72 explained, referring to school rules. "We were living in a fantastic country and we didn't know anybody except other Americans."[36] Linda Handschin-Sheppard '68 agreed. "[We were] quite restricted to Bliss and Hamra Streets," Sheppard remembered. "I did not get nearly as many opportunities to explore the country or the city as I would have liked."[37]

Potrezebie

In the late 1950s and early 1960s, Potrezebie became the unofficial mascot of the American Community School. The mascot was not a knight, as it would later become, but an ancient cannonball. A group of seniors "liberated" the cannonball from a castle in Tripoli sometime in the 1950s and named it "Potrezebie," which is a nonsensical word from Mad Magazine. The class of 1956 painted "Potrezebie" on the cannonball with the initials "GZ" – in honor of George Zarour, a popular science teacher.[38]

Mythology developed around Potrezebie. It became a symbol of "Senior Strength," as each graduating class passed the cannonball to the rising seniors in an elaborate ceremony in which the object was placed on a pillow between wooden bars and paraded around campus. Potrezebie was entirely a creation of the students, and the students therefore took special ownership of the new tradition. The mascot was also the subject of student newspaper articles and the recipient of pages of yearbook dedications. Students organized athletic competitions over which

Figure 6.9: The original Potrezebie, 1960

grade could take possession of Potrezebie.[39] The 1966 commencement address included inside jokes about the unofficial mascot.[40]

Eventually, the competition over Potrezebie got out of hand. Students broke into dorm rooms to steal the mascot. One student even carried Potrezebie in a bowling bag on a flight back to the U.S. Imitation Potrezebies appeared. Eventually, the symbolic mascot disappeared from the school and made its way to the ACS New York office where it resides to this day.

Arabic at ACS

In 1954, the Board considered the benefits of continuing Arabic and then decided to terminate the course. The record of these considerations offers insights about ACS in that era. "The chief advantage of Arabic teaching is its public relations value," the minutes read. "Most children in the school are in the Middle East only temporarily and a slight knowledge of Arabic is of no permanent benefit to them."[41] Clearly, the Board viewed the school as a temporary home for expats. But the decision to drop Arabic backfired. After a year without the language, a group of mothers petitioned successfully for the reinstatement of Arabic in the lower school.[42] Basic Arabic course were not offered again in the high school until the mid 1960s.

To this day, students from the early to mid 1960s express frustration that ACS did not provide them with an opportunity to learn Arabic. "I never had the chance to learn Arabic [at ACS]," explained Eleanor Dorman Johnson '62, who returned to Beirut in the 1990s. "Now that I am back here and living in Beirut, that is something that I regret."[43] Pieter Wybro '67 concurred. "One thing that I was disappointed in when I was going [to ACS] was that there weren't any Arabic classes."[44] Wybro's classmate, Philip Davies '67, found Arabic classes elsewhere.[45] Arabic was so important to Sam Constan '53, the son of an AUB professor, that he transferred to IC. Elizabeth Somerville Sadaka '60 chose not to send her children to ACS, her alma mater, because she wanted them to become proficient in Arabic.

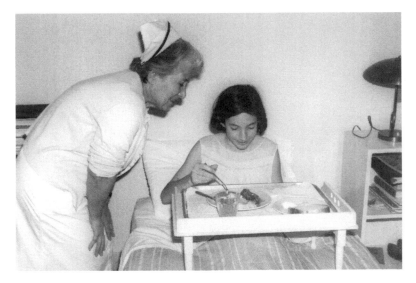

Figure 6.10: "Nursie" - Miss Haganoush Ipranossian and Patty Meade '70 in the infirmary of the Boarding Department, 1966

Bursting the Bubble

The Board, teachers, students and parents recognized that isolation was a problem. In 1956, soon after Arabic was removed from the curriculum, the Board considered ways to deal with the school's "reputation as a cultural island."[46] The Board offered a "Near East Culture" class, but the course failed after a year for lack of interest.[47] Students were criticized for their isolation in the school newspaper. "We are in one of the most interesting locations in the world," a student wrote in 1962. "However, most of us know only about Rue Bliss and Rue Hamra ... If we could break the wall of isolation that surrounds the school, we might enjoy ourselves. And in ten years, we might even miss Beirut!"[48] A preacher who was a guest speaker in chapel prodded students to take advantage of Beirut and break out of the "American shell."[49] In 1970, parents petitioned the Board "to explore greater integration with Lebanon."

During this period, there is evidence that the Board of ACS also recognized the need to expand their students' understanding of Lebanon by hiring Lebanese teachers. In 1953, the Board adopted the following policy:

> *In recognition of the need for an understanding and acceptance of the local culture on the part of the students, it will be the policy of ACS to employ a suitable proportion of local teachers, where qualified.*

The policy did not substantially change the proportion of Lebanese teachers to the overall faculty. In 1951, before the policy was adopted, 26 percent of the faculty members were Lebanese.[50] A decade after the policy went into effect, the percentage of Lebanese faculty declined to 18 percent.[51] In 1967, about one-fourth of the faculty was Lebanese.[52] Irrespective of the ratios, during this era, Lebanese teachers were the students' best window into the broader community.

ACS also created the Penrose Award to promote civic responsibility and, as a result, enhance the interaction of students with the Lebanese. The award, named in honor of a former AUB president, was given to the person "who has done the most to improve relations with the Lebanese."[53] Volunteer work offered the best opportunity for students to win the Penrose Award. Mrs. Churchill's entire 4th grade class won the award in 1967 for their work with the Lebanese poor.[54] Linda Handschin-Sheppard '68 worked in the refugee camps in South Lebanon "mixing cement or plaster in the heat."[55] In 1961, students raised funds to rent a bulldozer and helped construct a "Near East Boys Home" in a Palestinian refugee camp.[56] Monroe Pastermack '53 expressed a common sentiment of Americans who volunteered in the camps: he never forgot the experience of seeing, for the first time, true poverty.[57]

Despite the criticism of the "American ghetto," the experience of living in Beirut transformed the lives of many ACS graduates. In interviews conducted decades later, alumni explained that ACS changed their perspectives on the world: "I [understand] poverty and sickness because I saw lepers in the streets of Beirut; I saw the insane in the asylum; I went to the jails in Beirut," David Williams '74 said. "Since I interacted with other cultures at such a young age... I now feel for other cultures," he added.[59] For Camille Khatar Hedrick '70, "[Beirut] showed me that America is just one country. I can embrace different cultures. I can embrace different religions and I can debate about the issues in both America and elsewhere." Philip Davies '67 expressed the same feelings: "I noticed that when I came back to the U.S. and started interacting with these kids who went to school in Ohio, I felt somewhat broader than they did... I feel that perspective still with me."[60]

> "In the early 60s, Elias, Nimr Sammoun, Fawzi Bechara, Panos Havandjian and other staff were an essential part of the everyday of ACS. Nimr had his folding bed in a storeroom under the stair in the BD and set it up after 'lights out' squarely in front of the main door of the BD. That was his way of keeping us safe and that was his bedroom! Fawzi made everything work, Panos fed us, and Elias disbursed our infinitely important allowances - always with a smile. There were Ian Sellar, Margaret Anderson,[58] and others in the administration who smoothed the ripples and waves of everyday life. But the most loved must have been 'Nursie', Miss Haganoush Ipranossian. We dedicated the 1964 yearbook to her! "
>
> - Børre Ludvigsen '64

This and excellence in academics were the great gifts of ACS to its students. The school enabled them to see the United States and the world from differing perspectives. It prepared them academically and culturally for a return to the United States. Notwithstanding the "American ghetto" trend, ACS indeed exposed its students to a wider world.

The Six-Day War

Lebanon did not participate in what became known as the Six-Day War in June 1967. This war, principally involving Egypt and Israel, had a severe impact on Beirut as it suffered the volatility and fear that gripped the region.[61] When the war began on Monday, June 5, commerce in Beirut came to a standstill and the city went into an immediate nighttime blackout. On the day of the war's outbreak, anti-Israeli protesters held demonstrations outside of the U.S. Embassy and then moved towards AUB. Of larger concern, American interests in Lebanon became

Figure 6.11: Chris Baker '69 and Jack Harrison, 1967

targets of the violence. On the last day of the war, the Coca-Cola plant on the southern outskirts of Beirut was burned.[62]

ACS immediately took protective measures. The Board Chair, John Kelberer, and the headmaster, Jack Harrison, had developed contingency plans during the weeks of the buildup to the Six-Day War. By June 1, anticipating an outbreak of violence, Kelberer and Harrison instructed the school's boarders (numbering 180) and residency staff and dependents (numbering 66) to remain on campus. Harrison contacted the parents of boarders to address emergency plans in the event of an evacuation. Despite this, the school held its annual prom on June 3. Two days later the Six-Day War broke out and the school was evacuated.

The order for evacuation was delivered by the U.S. Embassy on June 5, 1967. "On June 5th at 4pm", recalled Sara Rich, "the BD staff met and were instructed that after dinner all the students in the BDs were to pack up their room as best they could and to prepare one suitcase that they could carry, a blanket, and some water. All of this was done in blackout conditions and in a calm atmosphere. The students were amazing! The plan was to gather all the boarders by the Boys BD entrance and go as a group to the AUB apartments open space from which they would be transported to the airport at first light to be evacuated on Pan Am flights which were arriving at daylight." During the week of the war, 4,500 Americans were evacuated from Lebanon; of these, the 180 ACS boarders were the first to leave.[63] Lunchtime at ACS was interrupted on Tuesday, June 6, by the sound of gunfire. By the afternoon, however, riot police had restored order and the Lebanese army posted a tank outside the ACS gate.[64] Some teachers evacuated on Wednesday, June 7, and others, like Wilfred Turmelle, the middle school principal, stayed in Beirut for the duration of the war.[65] The school facilities were essentially empty before the war ended, shortening the school year by three weeks. Thus, exams and commencement services were cancelled in 1967.

Figure 6.12: The 1967 evacuation

For the most part, students remember the 1967 evacuation as a time of excitement. "I was a 17 year old kid," Pieter Wybro '67 recalled. "This was really good stuff because I was getting out of school early."[66] The evacuations of June 1967 bore similarities to those of May 1941 and 1958. In all cases, students were happy to avoid final exams and to get an early start to the summer. Some viewed the conflict as an adventure. Within a day of the evacuation of the boarders, school families reported to either the airport or the seaport under guard of the Lebanese army.[67] From there they traveled by ship to places such as Marseille or by plane to Frankfurt. Other ACS community members sailed to Greece, where one teacher described the American refugee experience as an unexpected, but pleasant, tour of Athens.[68] Pieter Wybro '67 characterized his time in Greece as a series of "parties." Ultimately, there were few long-term negative effects of the 1967 evacuation. Seniors received their diplomas in the mail, and the school reopened the following September.

The ACS experience of the 1960s struck a balance between an education in the "American bubble" in Ras Beirut and real world exposure to one of the truly exciting Middle Eastern centers of commerce, politics and culture. Sometimes the comfort and security of isolation prevailed. However, on the whole, ACS graduates were forever changed by their experiences of living and attending school in Beirut. In hindsight, the 1960s witnessed the high point of the American identity of ACS. It was the Lebanese Civil War that ultimately jolted the school out of its "American ghetto."

Notes

[1] Bashshur [2005]; Alamuddin [2004]

[2] ACS [1964]

[3] Stacey [1997, p. 57]

[4] ACS Board of Trustees, May 28, 1959

[5] Stacey [1997, p. 57]

[6] Bashshur [2005]

[7] Azkoul [2005]

[8] Stacey [1997, p. 60]

[9] ACS Board of Trustees, May 7, 1970

[10] ACS [1963]

[11] ACS [1961a]

[12] Neff [Unknown year]

[13] ACS [d, 1961]

[14] McFeaters [2004]

[15] ACS [e, June 1955]

[16] ACS Board of Trustees, February 11, 1960; March 3, 1959

[17] ACS Board of Trustees, February 1, 1968

[18] ACS [e, June 1955]

[19] ACS [1963, p. 12]

[20] ACS [e, May 24, 1954]

[21] ACS [d, 1967]

[22] ACS [f, December 3, 1954]

[23] Tracy [2004]

[24] Stacey [1997, p. 40]

[25] ACS [1963]

[26] ACS Board of Trustees, May 22, 1963

[27] Stacey [1997, p. 46]

[28] ACS [1966-1967]

[29] Stacey [1997, p. 50]

[30] ACS [1961b]

[31] Tracy [2004]

[32] ACS Board of Trustees, January 23, 1953

[33] ACS Board of Trustees, December 5, 1957

[34] ACS Board of Trustees, October 18, 1963

[35] ACS Board of Trustees, November 27, 1963

[36] Atwood [2005]

[37] Handschin-Sheppard [2004]

[38] Stacey [2005]

[39] ACS [d, 1960]

[40] Barbir [1966]

[41] ACS Board of Trustees, September 14, 1954

[42] ACS Board of Trustees, June 30, 1955

[43] Johnson [2005]

[44] Wybro [2004]

[45] Davies [2004]

[46] ACS Board of Trustees, January 3, 1956

[47] ACS Board of Trustees, Pending Items for Consideration of the Board as Gleaned from the Minutes of 1959-1960

[48] ACS [c, Editorial. October 30, 1962]

[49] ACS [e, November 1953]

[50] ACS [d, 1951]

[51] ACS [d, 1964]

[52] ACS [d, 1967]

[53] ACS [d, 1964]

[54] ACS [1967]

[55] Handschin-Sheppard [2004]

[56] ACS [d, 1961]

[57] Stacey [1997, p. 44]

[58] Ian Sellar was Bursar and Margaret Anderson, the Headmaster's secretary.

[59] Williams [2004]

[60] Davies [2004]

[61] Kassir [2010, p. 469]

[62] Kassir [2010, p. 469]

[63] Lee [1968]

[64] Lee [1968]

[65] ACS Board of Trustees, September 26, 1967

[66] Wybro [2004]

[67] Porter [2004]

[68] Lee [1968]

7 New Norms of Behavior, 1968-1977

Figure 7.1: ACS film-makers at work - Ann Ratcliffe (science teacher), Richie Hanna, Vera Ellen Bernard, Jon Waterman, technician, January 1971

In some respects, little changed at ACS between the Six-Day War in 1967 and the outbreak of the Lebanese Civil War in 1975. Students of the late 60s and early 70s engaged in the same forms of entertainment as those of a decade or of a generation earlier – loud music in the dorms and gatherings at Kameel's, the local shop favored by students. Students were still engaging in pranks – tossing eggs from the roof of the high school building and "escaping" from their dorm rooms during after-hours with homemade ladders.[1]

Figure 7.2: James Ragland '67 and Elsa Turmelle in 1967, when she was still
guidance counselor

Most international members of the faculty had short tenures at ACS,
just as they had in the 1950s and 1960s. But ACS continued to attract engaging teachers (many of whom were very young) who motivated their
students. Hank Rigler, a new English teacher, established a reputation
for his demanding vocabulary quizzes. Dick Pellet trained students in
critical thinking – he encouraged them to disagree with him, as long
as they could support their positions with empirical information.[2] As
always, the Turmelles were a steady presence at ACS, and, appropriately,
they assumed more leadership responsibilities. By the late 1960s, Wilfred Turmelle was promoted to principal of the middle school and Elsa
Turmelle was appointed dean of students.

Despite the continuity, the years before the Lebanese Civil War posed
two new challenges. First, ACS experienced a decline in enrollment
for the first time since World War II. As Beirut increasingly gained a
reputation as a place of political instability, fewer American families sent
their children to the Boarding Department. The second challenge was a
more difficult one from which no educational institution was exempt:
drugs. Three factors or trends emerged at ACS from 1968 through 1975
to create extraordinary challenges in this second category. The first was
the growing use of drugs in America and changing societal attitudes
towards drug use. Secondly, illicit drugs were more readily available

Figure 7.3: Two of the most remembered and talked about teachers from the late 1960s and early 1970s: Peter Gibson, Ancient History teacher and dorm parent in 1969, and Dick Pellet, English, Geography and Theater Arts teacher

in Beirut than in most American cities. Hashish, LSD and prescription drugs could be bought and sold with relative ease by teenagers who had the money. Lastly, while an effective prefect system kept order and helped younger boarders adjust and develop positive leadership traits, boarders ultimately lacked the watchful eyes of parents who might have intervened more decisively.[3]

The administration and the Board struggled to control student behavior that, to some extent, was beyond the control and abilities of ACS or any school facing similar circumstances at the time.

A Struggle with Student Behavior

The realization that there was a drug problem at ACS dates back to December 1967. That month, Lebanese police arrested a drug dealer outside of Kameel's store, the most popular gathering place for ACS students. The dealer then gave the police the names of twenty American teenagers whom he claimed were his clientele. He also identified the products that he allegedly sold to the students. The police took the information to the Board of Directors of ACS.[4]

Following this very serious initial incident, school administrators and faculty discovered other cases of drug abuse and over the ensuing years expelled a number of students caught using drugs.

Parents, faculty and administrators struggled for solutions and remedies. School rules now clearly stated that any "use of toxic or habit-forming

Figure 7.4: Hank Rigler, English and Russian Literature teacher and football coach in 1970s, and Ray Ruehl who witnessed the early phase of the Lebanese Civil War

drugs" were "grounds for immediate expulsion."[5] Jack Harrison, the head of school, sought to deter drug use by banning attendance at "discothèques" such as the Locomotive and the Flying Coquette.[6] Yet students continued to use and get caught and parents continued to voice their concerns.[7] Harrison and the Board then tried an alternative approach. In 1970, ACS held an all-school assembly in which a doctor detailed the health risks associated with drug use. The faculty formed a committee to investigate the phenomenon, which included off-the-record interviews with students who were experimenting with drugs. The committee concluded: (1) Students primarily smoked hashish because they enjoyed it; (2) Prescription pills that were or would have been outlawed in the U.S. were easily available in Beirut's pharmacies; and (3) The fear of being caught was the greatest deterrent.[8] While there was no official change to the rules, ACS did adjust its punishments, and by 1974, the Board stopped expelling students for smoking hashish and instead placed them on disciplinary probation.[9]

Of course, the challenges of ACS were similar to those involving thousands of other high schools in the United States. America in the late 1960s and early 1970s witnessed a revolution in drug use and abuse – in effect, the "normalization" of drug use in American culture. Drugs became a dangerous rite of passage for American teenagers. But ACS was located only a mountain range away from the hashish farms of the Bekaa Valley, and it was in a community that lacked strict laws regu-

Figure 7.5: Students hanging out in 1974

lating use of prescription pills. This was a dangerous mix. In the end, there was one, and maybe only one, event that could suddenly reverse the student drug problems. That event was the Lebanese Civil War.

Declining Enrollment and Rising Tensions

For the five years leading up to the outbreak of the Lebanese Civil War in 1975, ACS witnessed a gradual decline in enrollment. The 1969-1970 school year marked the high point of the number of students: 1,010. The following year, 831 students attended the school, followed by 704 in the fall of 1971.[10] Fewer "oil kids" were attending ACS. In 1973, the children of Aramco/Tapline employees represented less than ten percent of the student population, compared to 40 percent a decade earlier.[11] In June 1973, fourteen students withdrew because of the "political situation," and the school was now operating at a deficit due to the decreasing enrollment. The successive years leading up to the Civil War set new highs for the school's annual budget deficits.[12]

In the spring of 1975 the fighting broke out. Ray Ruehl was in his eighteenth year as an art teacher. On the night of April 13, 1975, Ruehl and Margaret Anderson were dining at the Phoenicia Hotel. After dinner, they sensed that something was wrong as the streets were empty. The infamous "bus massacre" in an East Beirut suburb had just occurred. Militia groups throughout Beirut took to the streets, set up road blocks, and established sniper towers. After three days, 120 people had been killed. The Lebanese Civil War had begun.

Despite the turmoil of the emerging civil war, the American Community School never closed in the spring of 1975 although beginning in

Figure 7.6: Margaret Anderson (Headmaster's secretary) and student Jay Mc-Donald at the American Express office near the Holiday Inn hotel, March 1976

April, worried parents rushed to pull their children out of school. In June, when the Board first met after the commencement of hostilities, it decided not to cancel classes. The consensus was to stay in communication with the U.S. Embassy and to allow parents to decide whether it was safe for their children to attend school. The 1975 graduation ceremony and the prom were both held in these first few months of the war.[13] The fighting, it seemed, would only be temporary – as it had been in 1958. No one could have imagined that a cataclysmic civil war would last fifteen years.

The October Crisis

When school opened as scheduled in late September 1975, armed militias were still in the streets. On the way to school, students and families passed through roadblocks manned by young men with machine guns. Despite this, 537 students arrived on the first day of school. The Board reaffirmed its policy that it was "the responsibility of teachers and parents to determine individually the safety factor in coming to school each day."[14] For the first month of that school year, ACS was living a day-to-day existence.

Then the "hotel wars" began. In late October 1975, rival militias fought for control of the Holiday Inn which was a strategic location for snipers who could direct gunfire into the neighborhoods of opposing forces.

Figure 7.7: Evacuation - 1975-1976

Several ACS teachers lived in Ain el Mreisseh, a neighborhood just west of the Holiday Inn. Ray Ruehl was one of those teachers. "Ain el Mreisseh was quite safe or very dangerous depending upon who controlled the hotels," Ruehl wrote. "Boys with guns slung over their shoulders would come to the door and say 'Very dangerous today. Stay in. If you need anything we'll get it for you.'" On calmer days, the same boys would let the residents of Ain el Mreisseh go shopping. "It was as if the conflict was being choreographed and all the participants had scripts," Ruehl explained.[15]

By late October, it was clear that the teachers and students were in danger. On October 29, the Board voted to close the school for two weeks. Teachers living in Ain el Mreisseh were evacuated to the relative safety of the Boarding Department building. From the ACS campus, teachers watched shells land in the Mediterranean while sipping tea with colleagues.[16] During the two-week suspension, the U.S. Embassy advised all American citizens to leave Lebanon. ACS and American-owned companies complied, and ACS offered its American teachers one-way tickets home if they chose to leave.[17] When the school reopened on November 12, there were 98 remaining students. Over 400 students had evacuated. Thirty of eighty teachers remained.[18] Students and teachers (many of whom were longtime colleagues) left without the opportunity to say farewell. "When we came back to school [in November] there was no one there," remembered Laila Farah '81. "The halls were empty. There was a little handful of kids in each section and that diminished even more as time went by."[19]

Figure 7.8: Nimr Sammoun, Ray Ruehl, (unidentified), Panos Havandjian, and (unidentified) kitchen staff hiding out in the BD during the 'Troubles' in the late spring of 1976.

From October 1975 to May 1976, the few students who remained were assigned new schedules and new teachers. Students and teachers adjusted their routines and activities to the demands of war. Students scanned rooftops for snipers. They learned the difference between the noise of an exploding mortar shell and the sound of a military jet breaking the sound barrier.[20] Students routinely sought shelter in hallways, away from windows and incoming shrapnel. When the fighting ceased, middle school boys would scour neighborhoods for spent bullets and shrapnel.[21] Prior to playing tennis, students and teachers cleared the shrapnel from the school's courts.[22] Armed militiamen patrolled the streets outside of ACS while school was in session. During the 1975-1976 school year, ACS repeatedly was opened and then closed when the fighting intensified.

By April, only 69 students were attending ACS on a regular basis. The Board approved the recommendation of Robert Usellis, the headmaster, that ACS close several weeks early.[23] The graduation ceremony was abbreviated, but it was held on May 28, 1976. Six students received diplomas.

Surviving the 1976-1977 School Year

There were many reasons that the American Community School might have ceased to exist in the summer of 1976. One was the local militia that was a permanent presence in Ras Beirut. Squatters broke into the Boarding Department in search of a place to live. Robert Usellis was temporarily stranded in the United States. The school now had an accumulated deficit of $400,000, which was quadruple that of the previous year.[24] For budgetary reasons, ACS closed its Boarding Department, which ended a tradition of 55 years. In August 1976, Aramco/Tapline withdrew its sponsorship of ACS.[25] Thus ended a 30-year partnership that had transformed the school from a family-run institution into a boarding school with a regional reputation. Despite the militia, the break-ins, and the loss of Aramco funding, the Board of Trustees never considered closing ACS in the summer of 1976. When the 1976-1977 school year began, ACS had seventeen students and five full-time teachers.

Robert Usellis was able to return to Beirut, and he was vigorous in his support of the Board's decision that ACS not close. Wilfred and Elsa Turmelle were two of the remaining five faculty members. They took on more tasks, which included teaching outside of their areas of expertise and becoming de facto principals of the two divisions. The school leaders worked to boost enrollment and to provide its students with the best education possible.

Figure 7.9: Robert Usellis, head of school, 1971-1979

While Usellis and the Turmelles were struggling to maintain academic standards, the Board sought ways to make the school financially viable. ACS rented space to IC's elementary school. The Board voted to turn the Boarding Department into a youth hostel, which generated $30,000 in income. The school then received grants from the Ford Foundation, the Morgan Guaranty Trust Co., and the U.S. Embassy. Despite these efforts and successes, the budget deficit was $300,000 in the 1976-1977 year. Without more students, ACS would never be financially viable. Most American families were gone, and there were few other foreigners. The school had to find a new source of students.[26]

Once again, the American Community School turned to the Lebanese. On May 3, 1977, the Board changed to an open admissions policy. For over thirty years, the school had required special permission for the admission of non-American applicants. Now, the school actively sought and recruited Lebanese families. ACS was still not officially registered with the Lebanese government and it did not have the authority to grant Lebanese Baccalaureate diplomas. However, in the chaos of the war, ACS was one of the few English-speaking schools that remained open.[27] Primarily because of this, enrollment increased in 1977-1978 to 191 students.[28] ACS had survived the first period of the war.

The 1970s began with one challenge and then ended with another. At the beginning of the decade, ACS's administration struggled to respond to the problem of drug use among its student body. Hashish was commonplace and more than a dozen students were expelled for drug use between 1968 and 1973. But the problem persisted. The school adjusted its expectations and tried softer approaches involving flexible discipline and health education. In the end, the drug problem was dwarfed by the Lebanese Civil War.

The school survived the first two years of the war thanks to a small number of courageous and dedicated faculty, devoted trustees, and the head of school. These people saw it as their duty to provide an education for the few dozen students who could make it to school each day. The long-term survival of the school, the Board concluded in 1977, would depend upon the enrollment of English-speaking Lebanese students.

Notes

[1] Zughaib [2004]

[2] Ball

[3] Buckley [2012]

[4] ACS Board of Trustees, December 12, 1967

[5] ACS Board of Trustees, April, 1970

[6] ACS Board of Trustees, March 25, 1969

[7] ACS Board of Trustees, June 15, 1970

[8] ACS Board of Trustees, "Faculty Group Report on the Drug Problem.", May 14, 1970

[9] ACS Board of Trustees, May 30, 1974

[10] ACS Board of Trustees, July 8, 1972

[11] ACS Board of Trustees, February 4, 1973

[12] ACS Board of Trustees, November 29, 1974

[13] ACS Board of Trustees, June 5, 1975

[14] ACS Board of Trustees, October 2, 1975

[15] Ruehl [2010, p. 146]

[16] Ruehl [2010, p. 148]

[17] ACS Board of Trustees, October 29, 1975

[18] ACS Board of Trustees, November 16, 1975

[19] Farah [2004]

[20] Rogers [2004]

[21] Bailey [2010, p. 6]

[22] ACS [d, 1976]

[23] ACS Board of Trustees, April 22, 1976

[24] ACS Board of Trustees, January 20, 1976

[25] ACS Board of Trustees, August 19, 1976

[26] ACS Board of Trustees, May 10, 1977

[27] ACS Board of Trustees, May 3, 1977

[28] ACS Board of Trustees, October 20, 1978

8 A Day-to-Day Existence, 1978-1984

Figure 8.1: An ACS student blows off steam on the dance floor in 1979

During the military stalemate of the late 1970s, the school's annual enrollment stagnated at approximately 190 students and budget deficits continued. The conditions in Lebanon declined further in the late 1970s and early 1980s, and the challenges at ACS mirrored the general conditions in Lebanon. Between 1978 and 1984, ACS endured waves of evacuations of students and teachers. Enrollment was anemic and budget deficits accumulated. The leadership of the school passed from Robert Usellis to Elsa and Wilfred Turmelle. By 1984, the school was living a day-to-day existence, and it was constantly at risk of permanent closure.

The Low Point

From the outbreak of the Civil War, ACS faced dire conditions that required adaptation and perseverance. The Board increased tuition by 25 percent in an attempt to stem operating losses.[1] The tuition increase alienated parents and still did not balance the budget. As cost saving measures, the school no longer paid teacher stipends for coaching and after-school activities.[2] Stolen items ("victims" of the Civil War) were not replaced.[3] For five years, the school did not maintain its buildings, which resulted in leaking roofs, cracked windows, and peeling paint.[4]

The Israeli invasion of 1982 exacerbated the crisis. The invasion began on June 6, two weeks prior to graduation. A few weeks later, the Israeli army surrounded West Beirut and, according to Thomas Friedman of the New York Times, bombed the city "indiscriminately."[5] Elsa Turmelle cancelled classes and the prom. For the first time since 1967, ACS did not hold a graduation ceremony.[6] Three artillery shells hit the school's campus in the summer, which were the first direct military attacks of the war on the school. Fortunately there were no personal injuries.[7] When school opened in October, enrollment dropped from 192 students to 80. The Turmelles were required to reorganize classes, to recruit teachers, to replace departures, and to raise contributions. In Elsa's words, the curriculum was "a basic program, no frills." In the fall of 1982, there were no sports and no art classes. It was a challenge offering math and science to the few dozen students who remained.[8]

Also in the fall of 1982, several thousand U.S. Marines landed in Lebanon as a peacekeeping force. The arrival of the American soldiers in Ras Beirut was initially welcomed. In the first few months of the peacekeeping operation, students interacted with young Marines over sandwiches, and the Marines were delighted to see Americans so far from home.[9] Unfortunately, the American forces then became a target. On April 18, 1983, the U.S. Embassy was bombed. The embassy was less than a kilometer from the campus and more than 60 people died in the explosion. Curious students rushed towards the blast – not away from it.[10] In the aftermath of the attack on the embassy, ACS placed sandbags along the campus walls.[11] Children were not allowed to play on the athletic fields for fear of snipers.[12] The surrounding roads were

Figure 8.2: The scene of the 1983 U.S. Embassy bombing, the aftermath of which several ACS students witnessed.

barricaded to prevent car bomb attacks.[13] Kidnapping became a daily concern. As the school addressed security, in January 1984, Malcolm Kerr '49, President of AUB, was assassinated on the AUB campus. The Board began its meeting with a moment of silence in memory of their friend and colleague.

The low point for the school may have been in the late winter and spring of 1984. In February 1984, five artillery shells hit the high school building during school hours. The shells penetrated the library walls. Although there were 150 people in the high school building at the time, no one was hurt.[14] Students and faculty calmly followed safety routines by seeking shelter in the chemistry lab of the basement, but the psychological damage was severe.[15] More students left school. Even Catherine Bashshur, the Middle School social studies teacher who had been at ACS since 1964, left for the year.[16] In April 1984, an ACS parent was kidnapped.[17] He would not be the last. Later that month, an artillery shell landed on the Rabbit Field. The explosion blew out the windows of the gym and the high school building that surrounded the field. Fortunately, the incident occurred on a Saturday and no one was hurt.[18] When the 1983-1984 school year ended, only four seniors attended graduation. Over the summer, only two students remained enrolled at ACS.[19]

94

Figure 8.3: Damage from the February 1984 shelling at the back entrance to what was the Boarding Department infirmary

The Turmelles' Finest Hour

From 1978 through 1984, Elsa and Wilfred Turmelle led the effort to save ACS. The Turmelles had been an integral part of the school community for decades. When ACS created a separate division for the middle school in the early 1960s, Wilfred became its first principal. By the time the Civil War began, Wilfred had an extensive collection of birds which he would bring to class to lighten the mood.[20] He also could be quite reckless about his personal safety. During aerial bombings, when most ran to the basement, Wilfred might go to the roof with his binoculars. He was also known to take a lawn chair to the edge of the Green Line to watch the militias fight, as if he were watching a Fourth of July parade and fireworks display.[21]

Elsa was more sensible about her safety. In the 1950s, she began as a P.E. teacher but she quickly received much more responsibility. She was an organizer; she served as the athletic director, a guidance counselor, assistant principal, and finally, under Robert Usellis, as principal of the high school. When Robert Usellis left in the summer of 1979, the Turmelles moved into the Head of School apartment atop the BD. They were given a small pay increase, and Elsa became the de facto head

95

Figure 8.4: Elsa and Wilfred Turmelle, 1979

of school. Her title, however, never changed. From 1979 through the mid-1990s, ACS did not have an official head of school.[22]

Elsa and Wilfred Turmelle acted as principals, guidance counselors, deans of faculty, heads of security, classroom teachers, and landlords. Elsa Turmelle took on the responsibility of recruiting teachers including traveling to the U.S. during lulls in the fighting. In the spring of 1983, she struggled to find science and math teachers, and ultimately she engaged local ACS alumni and a few Peace Corps graduates to fill vacancies.[23] The Turmelles also assumed the duties of the school registrar, thereby assigning students to specific teachers and classrooms. They served as school guidance counselors, which of course included dealing with the emotional well-being of students traumatized in times of war.[24] Elsa Turmelle represented the school in its relations with the local militias in the area, and, in fact, the militias provided more protection against break-ins than the police.[25] Most importantly, the Turmelles were in charge of the safety of the ACS community. They made the final decisions on whether or not to cancel classes on a given day, or whether to cancel a drama production or the prom.[26] For assistance, Elsa kept in close contact with officials at the U.S. Embassy.[27] In fact, she had been at the Embassy six days before the Embassy bombing in April 1983.[28] Finally, Elsa Turmelle coordinated the Board's rental arrangements with the International College and with the College Louise Wegmann.[29] Ultimately, "Heads of School" is an insufficient title for the roles of the Turmelles at ACS from 1978 through 1984.

A Semblance of Normalcy

Ebba El-Hage joined ACS in 1982 as a young member of the elementary school faculty. According to Ebba, ACS was one of the few schools still hiring in the early 1980s. She remained at ACS for the next twenty years, and she eventually became the principal of her division. Her early unpleasant memories of ACS included: working behind sandbags, panic-stricken parents interrupting class to rescue their children after a bombing, and children crying at the sounds of gunfire. In an interview, she also reflected on how the community pulled together, especially at times of crisis. "We knew," Ebba explained, "that throughout the war, school was the only place where the children felt that life went on in a normal manner because at home there would be news reports, nervous parents, and shelling."[30]

Figure 8.5: Children playing in 1981 and lower-school students celebrate Halloween in 1984

Remarkably, there was an element of academic normalcy at ACS in the early 1980s, although the periodic dangers and disruptions altered school year objectives.[31] Teachers were required to improvise. But smaller classes did provide teaching advantages. Ronnie Hammad '81 recalled falling in love with literature in a class of eight students, because (among other things) he could not avoid his teacher's attention. His teacher employed Dostoyevsky's *Crime and Punishment* and John Steinbeck's *Grapes of Wrath* to provide Hammad with context to the war and misery around him.[32] Robert Foss, one of the last American teachers to leave Beirut, used rigor and good humor to teach French. The humor, in particular, helped ease the tensions that students bore.[33] Coach Ted Briggs still fielded a basketball team. He even organized a trip to Athens for an international tournament.[34] Drama productions continued despite shelling and power outages. "We had to perform in this ratty old theater with ceiling tiles falling down and no electricity," Laila Farah '81 remembered of the plays in which she performed. "Just getting the sense of being part of something productive and fun and creative – I think that we were really thirsty for that at the time."[35]

Figure 8.6: Anne Lockwood, 1980

Anne Christiansen Lockwood was one of the most beloved teachers of the early 1980s. She taught middle and high school English. She was a demanding educator who required her students to write and then re-write essays. She had the ability to detect the slightest imperfections in sentences, and she was prone to coat her pupil's essays with layers of red ink.[36] Lockwood was not only an excellent teacher of writing, she also had a passion for Shakespeare. She made *Macbeth* and *Romeo and Juliet* appealing to teenagers. Lockwood could get inside her pupils' minds, and she understood the world from their perspective, helping their points of confusion, and challenging them to do their best in extraordinarily challenging circumstances. Over thirty years later, Lockwood's students still speak about her with passion and endearment.[37]

The members of the ACS community socialized and developed bonds in ways that were unique to their times and that would have been unlikely during peacetime. Of course, there were many limitations on the social lives of students and faculty in the early 1980s. Also, the small number of students and teachers limited social interactions and made life seem especially constrained at times.[38] On the other hand, students had more free time during the day due to fewer classes. During lulls in the violence, students swam in the Mediterranean between classes. Some students neglected to attend class in favor of tanning on the rocky shore.[39] Kameel's was, as always, the popular gathering place. ACS lacked the administrative support and structure to prevent students from going to Kameel's during the school day, and students apparently took full advantage.[40] When there were unanticipated outbreaks of violence, students settled into routines such as remaining at each other's homes and exchanging guitar lessons while avoiding shelling in hall-ways and bathrooms.[41] If a school family lived in East Beirut, their children could be stranded for several days in Hamra with the families of classmates.[42]

Students and teachers lived their lives as best they could in the early 1980s. It took great effort and even courage to maintain a semblance of normalcy at school. The small things in life – discussing Dostoyevsky in an English class, competing in a basketball tournament, acting in a drama production, gathering with friends at a diner – became acts of resilience. Heidi Hilgendorf '85 captured the spirit. "There was just the few of us going through it every day and every day we were thrilled to see each other," Heidi explained. "You never knew if we would be back again."

The Decision

In the first months of 1984, the environment within which ACS was operating went from bad to worse. In February ACS came under direct fire during school hours and, when the school reopened, only twenty students remained. The first American hostage was taken captive a week later and the US Navy organized an evacuation of all American citizens.[43] It was within this context that the Board made one of the most important decisions in ACS history. In 1984 it approved the es-tablishment of a Lebanese Baccalaureate program. This allowed the school to attract qualified Lebanese students who did not hold a second nationality. This decision saved the school and dramatically changed the composition of the student body. When the Board made its decision to adopt the LB program, ACS had a budget deficit of almost $550,000.[44]

The decision to adopt the LB program was not a hasty one. As early as 1978, the school's lawyers had reviewed the legal ramifications of admitting students who only had Lebanese citizenship. Prior to the LB program, Lebanese-only students were required to sign a legal waiver acknowledging that ACS had no legal standing in the country.[45] Finally, in early 1984, the Board voted on three different options. The first was to continue the status quo: enroll as many students as possible and make up operating deficits by renting unoccupied facilities and applying for grants. This was the option advocated by Elsa Turmelle. The second was to close the school permanently, which meant that ACS would have to sell its property to pay back the hundreds of thousands of dollars of debt that had accrued since 1975. Given that property was selling for a third of its prewar value and the strong desire to keep the school open, this was neither a practical nor a desirable option.[46] Finally, ACS could change its identity. That would mean registering with the Lebanese government, adopting the official Lebanese curriculum and Baccalaureate, and recruiting Lebanese teachers and students.[47]

The final vote was divided, but those in favor of registering with the Lebanese government ultimately won. The board decided to create a fresh start by "terminating" all faculty contracts by June 1984.[48] Some teachers were "rehired," but the Turmelles chose to end their long careers at ACS and they returned to New Hampshire. The Board wrote in July 1984 that "Elsa Turmelle carried an extraordinarily difficult burden valiantly and very successfully and that the school would not be here now without her perseverance under very difficult conditions at ACS."[49] It was the end of an era.

The gamble on the LB program immediately paid off. The school's enrollment tripled in size, from 41 students in June 1984 to 121 in August 1985.[50] While there was no shortage of schools, many Lebanese preferred an American style education for their children and seized the opportunity to join the American Community School.[51]

Notes

[1] ACS Board of Trustees, September 22, 1978; ACS Board of Trustees, October 20, 1978

[2] ACS Board of Trustees, May 30, 1980

[3] ACS Board of Trustees, June 26, 1981

[4] ACS Board of Trustees, March 28, 1980

[5] Friedman [1989, p. 73]

[6] Stacey [1997, p. 65]

[7] ACS Board of Trustees, October 28, 1982

[8] ACS Board of Trustees, October 28, 1982

[9] Boustany [2012]

[10] Hilgendorf [2004]

[11] Stacey [1997, p. 64]

[12] Hilgendorf [2004]

[13] ACS Board of Trustees, November 6, 1983

[14] ACS Board of Trustees, February 15, 1984

[15] Boustany [2012]

[16] Stacey [1997, p. 64]

[17] ACS Board of Trustees, April 17, 1984

[18] ACS Board of Trustees, May 16, 1984

[19] Stacey [1997, p. 65]

[20] Nohos [2012]

[21] Bashshur [2012]

[22] ACS Board of Trustees, June 29, 1979

[23] ACS Board of Trustees, March 10, 1983

[24] ACS Board of Trustees, October 23, 1981

[25] ACS Board of Trustees, July 25, 1978

[26] ACS Board of Trustees, May 19, 1983

[27] ACS Board of Trustees, October 28, 1982

[28] ACS Board of Trustees, April 14, 1983

[29] ACS Board of Trustees, April 3, 1983

[30] El-Hage

[31] Abunnasr [2005]

[32] Hammad

[33] Abunnasr [2005]

[34] Stacey [1997, p. 64]

[35] Farah [2004]

[36] Boustany [2012]

[37] Buckley [2012]

[38] Abunnasr [2005]

[39] Farah [2004]

[40] Abunnasr [2005]

[41] Bailey [2010, p. 6]

[42] Abunnasr [2005]

[43] Stacey [1997, p. 58]

[44] ACS Board of Trustees, March 27, 1984

[45] ACS Board of Trustees, February 29, 1980

[46] ACS Board of Trustees, April 3, 1984

[47] ACS Board of Trustees, January 25, 1984

[48] ACS Board of Trustees, February 23, 1984

[49] ACS Board of Trustees, July 3, 1984

[50] Stacey [1997, p. 67]

[51] Zabad

9 ACS at War, 1985-1991

Figure 9.1: Catherine Bashshur, middle, with the Board of Trustees, 1985. George Zarour is first on the left

By the fall of 1984, Beirut was a city run by militias.[1] The civil war was in its tenth year. Israel had invaded two years earlier. The United States had intervened and then withdrawn. The leadership of the PLO had already been evacuated. Yet from 1984 through 1991, the conflict grew even more intense and complex. In 1986, for instance, militias in West Beirut—former allies—fought each other in what was called the "The War of the Camps." In February 1987, the Syrian army moved into Ras Beirut as a self-proclaimed peace broker, providing temporary stability that became known as the "Pax Syriana."[2] However, the kidnappings and assassinations continued. The United States government banned travel to Lebanon by its citizens in the spring of 1987.[3] In March 1989, the campus of ACS became ensnarled in crossfire between the Syrian army and General Michel Aoun's forces in East Beirut.[4] As one teacher described the spring, summer, and fall of 1989, "it was raining shrapnel every day."[5]

Meanwhile, ACS adapted, evolved, and ultimately survived. Upon her hiring in 1984, Bashshur received a mandate to recruit local students and to hire local teachers. A year later, the school officially submitted its application with the Lebanese government for accreditation.[6] The Board revised ACS's bylaws, deemphasizing the school's mission to educate American children and expressly establishing its goal to comply with Lebanese law.[7] After four years, on September 20, 1988, outgoing Lebanese President Amin Gemayel signed the decree recognizing the American Community School as a sanctioned school under Lebanese law.[8] By the end of the war in 1991, ACS could call itself both a Lebanese and an American school.

Catherine Bashshur's Leadership

Catherine Bashshur was from Pennsylvania and earned her master's degree in education from Florida State University in the late 1950s. She met her husband, Munir Bashshur, in Chicago in the early 1960s, and in August 1965, the Bashshurs married and moved to Beirut. ACS hired Catherine Bashshur to teach middle school social studies. She stopped teaching in the early 1970s to raise her children, but by the early 1980s she returned to ACS.[9] In February 1984, Bashshur evacuated to Cyprus with her teenage children for a few months. While she was in Cyprus, the Board solicited her application to be principal of ACS.[10]

There were over twenty other applicants for the position, and the Board narrowed its choice to two candidates. In the final interview, the other candidate emphasized maintaining academic excellence. Bashshur, on the other hand, recognized the extraordinary circumstances under which ACS was trying to survive. Yes, she would maintain high academic standards, but her emphasis was on the importance of creating a community for parents, teachers, and children. ACS needed to serve as a refuge from the war for the school community. It had to be an extension of the family in which every member supported each other in the effort to survive each day. Relationships, more than academics, would help ACS survive the crisis.[11] The board unanimously selected Bashshur as the new leader of ACS.[12]

Enrollment was the most pressing challenge for Bashshur when she took over in August 1984. Only 41 students were enrolled for the upcoming school year.[13] The Lebanese Baccalaureate program had yet to receive accreditation from the Lebanese government. Parents of high-school students were required to sign acknowledgments that their children's degrees from ACS would not be recognized in Lebanon, which obviously was a major deterrent for local families.[14] So Bashshur focused her energies on recruiting younger families with children in the elementary school. She also worked with Eileen Knight, the elementary school principal, to create an "early years program." By the time that these young Lebanese students reached high school, Bashshur hoped, ACS would have an LB program to offer.[15]

The strategy paid off. By opening day 1985, enrollment had increased to 175 students.[16] The following year, the school again doubled in size, and again in 1987. By 1989, nearly 600 students were enrolled at ACS.[17] It was a "bottom-heavy" school, with a disproportionately young student body.[18] For instance, in each of the school years from 1984 through 1989, over two-thirds of the students were in the elementary or early years programs.[19]

Figure 9.2: Catherine Bashshur, with teachers and students from the Class of 1988, in her apartment

Despite the increasing enrollment, money was always in short supply. Above all, the school needed funds to repair its buildings. In the winter of 1984, the high school building suffered $400,000 in damages from direct hits.[20] The money that would have been used for routine maintenance was used to repair broken windows and fill in holes from shrapnel. Without maintenance, buildings and infrastructures deteriorated. Bashshur estimated that ACS needed an additional $400,000 to replace all of the piping in the BD building.[21] To add insult, in 1987 USAID reduced its grant money to the school.[22] Bashshur scrambled for funds. She negotiated a 25 percent rent increase with IC and the

College Louise Wegmann, who were still renting space.[23] She returned to the United States each year to solicit annual gifts from alumni, flying from San Diego to New York City.[24] She applied for grants from the Hariri Foundation.[25] These efforts were essential in order to keep ACS affordable for its families who were suffering their own financial struggles in the midst of war.

Bashshur also rallied the Board of Trustees. George Zarour, a former teacher at ACS, was the first Chair under whom Bashshur served. In the 1950s, Zarour was a beloved science teacher. After leaving ACS, Zarour earned a PhD and became a professor at AUB. In 1984, he was elected Board Chair of ACS, which was the culmination of remarkable rise from an employee of the school to its Chairman. He was also the first Lebanese Board chair.[26] However, in 1986 Zarour stepped down from the board due to the stresses of the war. In the summer of 1985, the Board's secretary, Zahi Khuri, was kidnapped and never found. George Miller, another member of the Board, had his life threatened and fled that same year. In September 1986, Joe Cicippio, the Board's treasurer, was kidnapped and would be held captive for five years. In March 1987, Reverend Farr resigned from the Board and fled the country.[27] That left the Board with only two members, which was insufficient for a quorum and in violation of the rules established by the school's charter.[28]

With the majority of ACS's trustees kidnapped or in exile, the Board moved to New York City, which generated another challenge for Bashshur. With the relocation of the Board in the spring of 1987, she lacked a key network of support in Beirut. Her trustees were thousands of miles away, and they met only a few times a year. Bashshur was now required to fly to the U.S. in unsafe conditions three times a year. She lost the benefits of "hands on" consultation and support from these experienced leaders in times of extraordinary emergencies. Bashshur also had to assume the efforts to obtain Lebanese accreditation. She had to deal with a series of lawsuits with renters of ACS property.[29] She authorized an increase in tuition by 185 percent and in teacher pay by 225 percent in order to keep up with the massive depreciation of the Lebanese currency.[30] In peacetime, Heads of School were able to include the Board in the decision making process. This was impossible for Bashshur, as she was only able to advise her distant Board of her decisions after the fact.

Notwithstanding the international communication and travel demands, Bashshur's feet were firmly planted in Beirut with daily life at ACS. She maintained relations with the neighborhood militia, the Progressive Socialist Party (PSP). Many of these young men, who were openly armed with AK-47s, were the same ages as some of her students.[31] At times, they posted snipers in the buildings surrounding ACS. At times, militias exchanged gunfire over the heads of children playing on the athletic field.[32] During extreme bombings, Bashshur allowed the militia onto campus to seek shelter. She even remembers them playing pick-up basketball games in the school gym during the periodic bombings.[33] Yet at other moments there was tension with the local militia, such as in November 1986, when the militia entered ACS uninvited, fully armed and in combat fatigues. They went from room to room, carrying their AK-47s and rocket-propelled grenades, ripping down Lebanese and American flags.[34] Bashshur later learned that the militia had been storing its weapons in the basement of the gym.[35] There was little that Bashshur, or anyone else, could do at that point.

Figure 9.3: Students celebrate halloween and Christmas, 1988; despite the war, holiday traditions continue.

Bashshur also had to deal with discipline problems among her own students. Missing classes was the most common discipline offense during the war years – an obvious outgrowth of war and chaos. Bashshur was a master at employing shame and guilt as a mean as of discipline. She would appear in the doorway at Kameel's and without saying a word, with just a look, teenagers scampered back to class. But there were much more serious disciplinary issues, such as when a student brought an AK-47 to ACS to sell to a classmate. In another incident, a student brought a hand grenade to school and rolled it down the hallway as a prank. Bashshur calmly confiscated the hand grenade and left it on a shelf in her office until it could be disposed of.[36]

Above all, Bashshur loved her students, and the students returned her affection in kind. They considered her a surrogate mother. Through her leadership and forceful personality, ACS became an extension of each student's family. She accomplished this while articulating a new vision for the school. "ACS will be a first rate, high quality, bi-cultural, bilingual school community for both American and Lebanese," Bashshur wrote in 1986. "Both sides will draw on the strong points of one another to create a type of school that does not exist anywhere in Lebanon."[37] ACS's new leader embraced the new dual identity of the school as an inherently positive change, not just as a necessary wartime adjustment.

The Teacher's Perspective: Daily Struggles and Relentless Anxiety

From 1984 through 1991, ACS's faculty became younger and more Lebanese. American teachers had been fleeing Beirut since 1975, and by 1987, they were forced to leave by order of the U.S. State Department. In the spring of 1987, Secretary of State George Schultz decreed that no U.S. citizen could travel to or reside in Lebanon using U.S. documentation. With that decree, the last two American teachers at ACS – Eileen Knight and Robert Foss – left the school for good.[38] For nearly a decade thereafter, the only American teachers at ACS were dual passport holders. The few foreign teachers were Canadian.[39] Thus, Bashshur relied heavily on young Lebanese teachers, many of whom were straight out of college. She preferred younger teachers because she believed that they could be "molded into American-style educators" as opposed to the French style more common in Lebanon. By the end of 1987, the average age of a teacher at ACS was 24.[40]

Completing the basic tasks at ACS in the 1980s became a daily challenge. Driving to work, for example, could be life threatening. "If a militiaman did not like your religion or the last name on your I.D. card, it could all be over," recalled Nada Aoun, who worked in the business office.[41]

Figure 9.4: Robert Foss and Eileen Knight were the last American teachers to leave ACS during the Lebanese Civil War

For Haifa Hijazi, the librarian, cleaning up shrapnel in the library was part of her routine. Because the library was on the top floor, it would fill with hot metal penetrating the roof.[42] When teachers arrived at work, they did not know if they would complete the day or stay for just a few hours. The teachers prepared academic packets so that students could complete their studies from home.[43] When the shelling lasted for extended periods of time, the teachers improvised with correspondence courses. On such days, students and parents would pick up their work during pauses in the shelling and then return home to continue their studies in makeshift bunkers and basements. Teachers, meanwhile, had to be at school to coordinate the activities, photocopy materials and grade completed work. As Bashshur noted in a report to the board, ten teachers took on the work of sixty during these times.[44]

The constant shelling, gunfire, and explosions took their toll on teachers. Catherine Bashshur recognized this when she wrote the following in 1990:

> *The continuous shelling throws some adults into a panic while others, not visibly frightened, move about and go through the motions of work without being able to accomplish much – their minds cannot function on the abstract level, survival is all that is important. Questions like food, shelter, and location of loved ones is all that is foremost in their minds.*

Bashshur's description is supported by the recollections of her teachers nearly thirty years later. Maysa Boubess, at the time the director of the preschool program and currently an elementary school teacher, suppressed her fears as deeply as possible in order to avoid frightening her pupils.[45] Haifa Hijazi, ACS's librarian, was "always on my last nerves" and in a state of hyperactivity, constantly on the move.[46] Above all, teachers remember the horrible feeling of not being able to assure the safety of their students. The relentless anxiety was exhausting.[47]

The Student's Perspective: Freedom, Confinement, and Fear

The demographics of the student body mirrored that of the teachers – it was younger and more Lebanese. As previously indicated, the student body was younger because the school had actively sought to increase enrollment in its early years and elementary school programs. From 1984 through 1989, over two thirds of the students were in the fifth

Figure 9.5: Maysa Boubess (left), 1988. In the left corner of the photograph, sandbags cover the window to Boubess' office. A father picking his son up (right), 1988

grade or earlier. In 1986, 76 percent of ACS's students were enrolled in elementary school while just 15 percent were enrolled in high school. Meanwhile, more and more Lebanese students joined the ACS community. In 1982, there were few, if any, solely Lebanese students, as the majority of the student body held dual citizenship. That quickly changed as the 1980s progressed. In 1986, 66 percent of the student body was solely Lebanese. Three years later, nearly 80 percent of the student body was Lebanese.

Life for teenagers at ACS was a bit of a paradox. On the one hand, the war brought more freedom during school hours. Students smoked on campus. They rode their motor bikes into the courtyard and in circles on the Rabbit Field.[48] Due to the sporadic shelling, it was difficult to keep track of students during the day. It was not unusual for a student to leave in the middle of class without objection from the teacher.[49] Kameel's became an unofficial student lounge. During free periods, students played pinball at Kameel's while hiding from the occasional teachers trying to find them.[50] They would also interact with armed militiamen there. They played soccer with members of the PSP and even became friends with the armed teenagers. Through these interactions, students occasionally brought weapons onto campus, including the infamous grenade incident.[51]

On the other hand, ACS students bore overwhelming feelings of confinement. Most students rarely traveled beyond the neighborhood. "Bliss

Figure 9.6: Ebba El-Hage (left), director of the lower school. First graders (right), 1988

Street, AUB's campus, and ACS – that was my world," John Nohos '88 recalled.[52] While ACS lacked the administrative structure to keep track of students during the day, students were confined to their apartments and basements at night. The father of Anna Salameh Boustany '84 hired a guard to escort Anna from school back to their apartment on Bliss Street. If school ended at 3:20, Anna was to be home promptly at 3:25.[53] Students could not go to the movies at night. They could not go out to dinner on Hamra Street. Many grew up without setting foot near downtown or in East Beirut, which were just a few kilometers away.[54] Their social lives consisted of spending the night at friend's houses during rounds of shelling. Going to Bliss Street for ice cream was a thrill.[55] Life was confined to school, where a semblance of normalcy could be created, and to the basement of apartments, where electricity and water were a luxury and where students studied by candlelight with explosions erupting outside. "It was like jail," one student recalled.[56]

ACS students grew up with uncertainty and fear as a part of their daily existence – by the mid to late 1980s, that was all that ACS students could remember. At times, they were caught in firefights among rival militias. One time, a group of lower-school students hid behind the athletic field wall, unsupervised, with bullets flying overhead, until a teacher came to their aid during a break in the shooting.[57] Elementary school students cried hysterically at the slightest disruption. The emotional strain sometimes took on physical forms. One child vomited every time he heard a loud banging noise.[58] There were moments when shells landed near the elementary school playground during school hours.[59] Catherine Bashshur remembered one shell landing in front of Kameel's while students were relaxing inside.[60]

Figure 9.7: Students from the Class of 1988 celebrate graduation

Some of the most memorable experiences of the war generation involved their few opportunities to escape the confines of Ras Beirut. One of the highlights of John Nohos' high school life was skipping school as a junior and driving to the Chouf with two friends. They spent the day firing AK-47s and rocket-propelled grenades, something that Nohos now considers "incredibly stupid." But for a teenager whose life had been confined to a few square blocks in Ras Beirut, the experience was liberating.[61] The class of 1990 participated in a "Senior Skip Day" three years later. By that point, the fighting had died down. For a group of seventeen and eighteen year-olds with no memory of Lebanon before the war, taking a day off from school to drive to the mountains was an unprecedented adventure. "We just didn't have enough space to express ourselves," Malek el Jisr '90 wrote years later. "To go out from Beirut with no plans made us feel we had achieved a kind of happiness and freedom that could have only happened with that skip day."

1989: "It was raining shrapnel"

At 7:25 a.m. on March 14, 1989, General Michel Aoun declared a war of liberation against Syria. Five minutes later the shelling started. Salem Abu Hadba, an ACS senior, was on his way to school at 7:45 a.m. when a shell hit his car in the intersection in front of UNESCO. Salem was killed, and the car was burned beyond recognition. Fourteen hours passed before his parents learned of what happened when they arrived on ACS's campus at 10:00 p.m. that night looking for him.[62] Salem, who was of Jordanian descent, was a brilliant mathematician but also quite mischievous, according to Catherine Bashshur. He was suspended the day he was killed, and he was on the roads because he wanted to see friends before school began. Salem's friends and teachers at ACS had loved the young man. Catherine Bashshur says that she still has not recovered from his death, which was a devastating blow to the close-knit ACS community.[63] Salem was the only ACS student to be killed during the war.

Figure 9.8: ACS teachers prepare packets during a break in the shelling, 1989

Salem's death marked the beginning of the school's darkest and most dangerous period. From March 1989 through October 1989, the school was caught in the crossfire between the Syrian army, which had occupied the neighborhood since 1987, and Michel Aoun's forces in East Beirut. When the shelling began, the Syrians had already occupied the athletic fields for over a year. They placed a 40 millimeter gun on the rooftop of the building next to the elementary school, and they patrolled the neighborhood with heavy guns mounted on trucks. The main Syrian batteries were located four blocks west of the campus, so some of the incoming shells that fell short of their targets landed on the school. Once the shelling began, the Syrian army moved into ACS's gym and high school. The soldiers placed armored personnel carriers on the west side of the Boarding Department and high school buildings to shield their equipment from incoming shells from the east.[64] Thus, the school buildings served as bunkers for the Syrian army, or, as Catherine Bashshur described it, the campus was part of a metaphorical volleyball net with shells passing overhead and shrapnel raining down.[65]

The shelling was incessant during that eight month period in 1989. "The shrapnel fell everywhere, you didn't know where to hide," explained Haifa Hijazi.[66] Since the Syrians occupied the gym and high school building, school operations were crammed into the Boarding Depart-

Figure 9.9: Plant maintenance was a struggle - ACS's gym after the Syrians evacuate in 1989

ment and elementary school buildings. Hot metal came through the roof and through the sides of the building, lodging into the floors and walls. "Sounds of guns are ear splitting, bone jarring, and nerve racking," Catherine Bashshur wrote to the Board at the time.[67] The sound was so deafening that the vibrations cracked the mortar of the building – needless to say, the windows shattered and were replaced with sandbags. Despite the fact that electricity and water were cut off, six families continued to reside in the Boarding Department building, including the Bashshurs and Nada Aoun's family.[68]

Remarkably, the school remained open. Each day, during pauses in the shelling, teachers made their way to campus. They went about their routines – photocopying materials, preparing packets of worksheets that students worked on while seeking shelter at home, and grading the returned materials. Students and parents made daily trips to ACS to pick up the work. Because phone lines were down, people communicated through word of mouth. Teachers were available to meet with students from around 9:00 a.m. to noon, when the shelling was typically the lightest. In essence, ACS operated a series of correspondence courses in the summer and fall of 1989 while maintaining the school's standards for promotion.[69] In order to advance to the next grade, students not only had to complete their work from home but also pass a final exam. Final

Figure 9.10: A Syrian soldier observes graduation in the mid-1980s

exams came in a break in the fighting during July. Only five students met the requirements for graduation that year.[70]

As Catherine Bashshur described it at the time, ACS "limped through" the 1989-1990 school year. The shelling slowed in October 1989; the Syrian army withdrew from the gym, and 355 students attended the first day of classes. For the first time in eight months, students and faculty could attend classes on a regular basis, although the fighting in Beirut was not yet over. In January 1990, Maronites fought Maronites in East Beirut, with an occasional wayward shell landing near the school. The son of an employee was killed by a land mine that winter. Two stray bullets came through the windows of the high school auditorium during school hours. As the war wound down, the school community seemed to suffer from post-traumatic stress disorder. Students were easily agitated and struggled adjusting to school life. Teachers were irritable and short tempered. Catherine Bashshur even admitted that, despite the relative peace that year, "morale dropped to zero." They did not realize it at the time, but ACS had survived the Lebanese Civil War.[71]

Peace and Renewal

The 1990-1991 school year witnessed a resurgence. As an uneasy peace settled across Lebanon, two conflicts outside of the country brought an influx of new students. A civil war in Liberia led to an exodus of Lebanese expatriates living in West Africa. Second, in August 1990, Saddam Hussein invaded Kuwait, which caused much of the Lebanese population in the Gulf to return home. The result was an enrollment of 670 students, nearly double the number from the previous year.

With ACS now offering the full Lebanese Baccalaureate program, local families who sought an American-style education no longer hesitated to send their children to the school. During this 1990-1991 school year, ACS held 172 days of classes, a record during Catherine Bashshur's tenure at that point. Students went on field trips to Byblos and Beited-dine for the first time since before the war. Sports tournaments were held with rival schools from across Lebanon. Normalcy was returning to ACS life.[72]

Why did the teachers and administrators remain at ACS and in Beirut under such terrible conditions between 1984 and 1991? For some, the issue was, in part, financial. Several teachers did not have the money to leave the country and to start over. For others, there was a burning desire to remain in Beirut – and to never become a refugee. Beirut was their home. Many faculty from the 1980s explained that a sense of duty to the students kept them in Beirut – the students needed them.[73]

And then there was Catherine Bashshur. She explained that, notwithstanding the violence, she loved her life in Ras Beirut. Bashshur loved her colleagues, her students, and the broader community. She enjoyed the daily challenges of running a school, and balancing the interests of the Board, the faculty, and the parents. Plus, Bashshur admitted twenty years after the war, "I am extremely stubborn." Leaving was not an option. It was that simple.[74]

Notes

[1] Nohos [2012]

[2] Bashshur, May 1988

[3] ACS Board of Trustees, February 6, 1987

[4] Bashshur, June 1989

[5] Hijazi [2012]

[6] ACS Board of Trustees, August 6, 1985

[7] ACS Board of Trustees, June 5, 1986

8 al-Jaridah al Rasmiyah al [September 20 1988]

9 Bashshur's title was originally "Principal of ACS" The Board did not change her title to "Head of School" until the mid-1990s. When asked about the different titles in a 2012 interview, Bashshur responded, "I didn't pay any attention to that."

10 Bashshur [2012]

11 ACS Board of Trustees, August 1, 1984

12 ACS Board of Trustees, August 7, 1984

13 ACS Board of Trustees, October 4, 1984

14 ACS Board of Trustees, November 27, 1984

15 Bashshur, February 1987

16 ACS Board of Trustees, October 30, 1985

17 Bashshur, June 1989.

18 Bashshur [2005]

19 Bashshur, June 1989

20 ACS Board of Trustees, August 7, 1984

21 Bashshur, June 1990

22 Bashshur, February 1987

23 ACS Board of Trustees, June 5, 1985

24 ACS Board of Trustees, June 14, 1985

25 ACS Board of Trustees, October 30, 1985

26 ACS Board of Trustees, October 4, 1984

27 Bashshur, May 1988

28 ACS Board of Trustees, October 4, 1984

29 Bashshur, February 1987

30 Bashshur, May 1988

31 Nohos [2012]

32 Chapman [2012]

33 Bashshur [2012]

34 Nohos [2012]

35 Bashshur [2012]

36 Nohos [2012]

37 Bashshur, August 1986

38 ACS Board of Trustees, February 7, 1986

39 Alamuddin [2012]

40 Bashshur, February 1987

41 Aoun [2012]

42 Hijazi [2012]

43 Boubess [2012]

44 Bashshur, June 1989

45 Boubess [2012]

46 Hijazi [2012]

47 Boubess [2012]

48 Mihdahi [2005]; Boustany [2012]

49 Boustany [2012]

50 Boustany [2012]

51 Nohos [2012]

52 Nohos [2012]

53 Boustany [2012]

54 el Jisr [2010, p. 182]

55 Nohos [2012]

56 Boustany [2012]

57 Chapman [2012]

58 Boubess [2012]

59 Boubess [2012]

60 Bashshur [2005]

61 Nohos [2012]

62 Bashshur, March 1989

63 Bashshur [2005]

64 Bashshur, June 1989

65 Bashshur, May 1990

66 Hijazi [2012]

67 Bashshur, June 1989

68 Aoun [2012]

69 Bashshur, June 1989

70 Bashshur, May 1990

71 Bashshur, May 1990

72 Bashshur, July 1991

73 Boubess [2012]

74 Bashshur [2005]

10 Rebirth, 1992-2003

Figure 10.1: ACS faculty on a tour of the "Green Line" in 1994

During the Lebanese civil war, Catherine Bashshur had articulated a new vision for ACS whereby it would become a truly bi-cultural institution. With the restoration of peace in the early 1990s, the school finally had the opportunity to achieve Bashshur's vision.

The ensuing contradictions in educational philosophies and cultural clashes, and the need to reconcile the bi-cultural paradox fell to a core group of young teachers. This group, hired in the wake of the war, was part of the lost generation of Lebanese; They spent their formative years in the midst of war or fleeing from it in exile. These young teachers, themselves denied a stable education by the war, rebuilt ACS and strived to maintain an American institution within a Lebanese context.

The Challenge: "Catching up with the rest of the world"

In June 1992, Bashshur reflected on the war and on ACS's future. "For years the city, and the school being part of that city, have been satisfied with survival until the next day, week, or year," she wrote. "Now that the fear of destruction from violence is passing, we have time to look around and see what we need to do to catch up with the rest of the world."[1] The next ten years was the story of ACS catching up with the rest of the world.

Figure 10.2: A "dusty campus;" the Rabbit Field prior to its renovation

The physical reconstruction of the school was perhaps the first and most pressing concern. Central heating broke down in the winter of 1992. It was so cold that year that classes could not be held on the first floor.[2] In 1994, piping in the elementary school building burst and had to be replaced, and the Boarding Department building had to be renovated so that 24 faculty families could live there comfortably.[3] USAID helped pay for new science labs in 1995. During the war, the school had been reduced to having one lab from at least two before the war: one for biology and the other for chemistry.[4] In the mid-1990s, ACS finally installed some air conditioning, a computer lab, and functioning lavatories – all things that private schools take for granted.[5] Other problems were beyond ACS's control. Periodically, Beirut's city pipes would burst, leaving the school without water and without the ability to fix the problem.[6] Finally, by the late 1990s, the school began to beautify the campus. The goal was to make ACS a park-like setting, or an "urban oasis." To do that, trees and plants were planted in various parts of the campus. In 2005, the Rabbit Field was transformed from a dusty patch of dirt to what now seems like a garden.

The physical reconstruction of the school took place in the midst of ongoing disruptions and chaos. AUB's College Hall, for instance, was bombed in November 1991, destroying a building more than a century old. The attack on AUB, which occurred a year after the war was supposed to have ended, caused physical as well as psychological damage to ACS. The blast threw ACS's doors out of alignment, broke windows, and sent debris onto the elementary rooftop playground. More importantly, many teachers and students with close links to AUB felt "personally violated" by the attack.[7] "It was traumatic because it was our college, the college that was trying to do so much for this country," Dania Maaliki, an ACS teacher and AUB graduate, explained. "It wasn't about politics. We felt like they were trying to destroy education."[8]

Figure 10.3: The addition of the fourth floor library in 1998

There were other incidents that created feelings of instability. In April 1992, the Lebanese pound plunged in value; school employees watched helplessly as their salaries were effectively cut in half by the depreciation of the currency.[9] In May 1992, the school closed for two days due to protests and riots. Four years later, Israel's Grapes of Wrath campaign in south Lebanon led to a flood of refugees into Beirut and a loss of electrical power throughout the city.[10] In October 1997, a motorist on

119

the Corniche threw a bomb, perhaps dynamite, over the AUB perimeter wall. The explosion shattered the windows of the nearby ACS elementary school and knocked out the Boarding Department windows facing north. Ibrahim Bedeir, head of ACS's physical plant, called his staff at 10 p.m. that evening. The staff worked through the night, cleaning up every shard of glass before school began at 8 a.m. By the end to the school day, the windows had already been replaced.[11] No classes were interrupted. ACS kept moving forward.

Figure 10.4: Students in the new library, 1998

Despite the successes with the physical reconstruction of the school, there was psychological damage from the recent war and the continued threat of violence. In the early 1990s, children were still traumatized by the war – once, a group of youngsters cried hysterically at the sight of Halloween masks. The school hired counselors in 1992 to help elementary school students grapple with their post-trauma struggles. There was community-wide therapy in which students drew pictures to express their feelings.[12] But it was the adults, perhaps even more than the children, who were grappling with the remnants of the war. Many never believed the fighting was truly over and assumed violence could erupt again at any moment. "The issue was whether or not we could wake from the trance of war," explained ACS science teacher Samer Madbak. "I remember asking myself in 1995, 'Is the fighting actually over? Do we live day to day or do we start to plan long term?'"[13]

A Distant Board

ACS's Board of Trustees did not meet in Beirut for more than eleven years, from 1987 until 1998. Trustees were not to blame for the separation; the U.S. State Department forbade travel to Lebanon on American passports. The fact remained, however, that the trustees were isolated in New York City, and they struggled to maintain a link with their school. Ultimately, Walter Prosser, a trustee who had only visited the school once in his life, took it upon himself to grapple with the financial, legal and managerial difficulties caused by the Board's isolation.

In 1993, an accreditation team visited ACS to analyze the myriad of challenges facing the school. There was one issue that the accreditors focused on above all else – the Board's separation from the school:

> *The Board appears to have lost the kind of contact with the school that a Board ought to have; and the school has lost touch with the Board. As always, when this happens the Board may also have lost touch with itself.*[14]

The accreditation team had high praise of the "talent and resolve" of Catherine Bashshur, calling her "heroic... equal to every exigency... with every crisis producing a new strength." The report concluded that "rarely does an evaluative commentary rise to this level of praise." Yet, the accreditors subtly reprimanded the Board for failing to help Bashshur in her efforts. "Development policy is something only the Board can provide," they wrote. "At the present time there are no development goals. There is no strategic or long-range plan, and the future of the school is uncharted."[15]

Walter Prosser tried to fill the vacuum caused by the Board's distance. Prosser, a former intelligence officer for the U.S. Army in the Middle East, was a slight man with a thick mustache who wore large glasses and a bowtie.[16] He was also a scholar and a consummate reader with years of experience working for American institutions in the Middle East. He previously was director of the Near East College Association, which was affiliated with AUB, IC, Robert College in Turkey, and also ACS.[17] Yet Prosser was neither an ACS alumnus nor a former parent; he had only visited the school once in the 1980s prior to the travel ban. Despite his lack of personal ties to ACS, Prosser helped save the school in the wake of the civil war.[18]

Prosser joined the Board in the 1980s almost by default – he was one of the few in New York who had an interest in helping the Beirut school. By

Figure 10.5: Walter Prosser in the 1980s

the early 1990s, Prosser recognized that the ACS Board was a "makeshift outfit" and, due to the circumstances, had been forced to break with "80 years of tradition of having its board in Beirut."[19] Prosser was also vocal in his support for Bashshur. He went on record at several meetings, arguing that Bashshur needed more support from the Board in setting long-term goals, investing in capital campaigns, building an endowment, and fundraising with alumni of ACS.[20]

Prosser became ACS's eyes and ears in North America. He wrote monthly memoranda to the Board members, coordinated meetings, and lobbied the State Department to lift its ban on travel to Lebanon.[21] He organized the effort to obtain financing for ACS and corresponded with Beirut landowners willing to sell property to the school.[22] He met with US-AID officials to negotiate a $400,000 grant and was in contact with the Lebanese Ministry of Education.[23] Prosser took the time to respond to each letter of complaint or concern, whether about tuition, homework load, or changes in the curriculum.[24] Throughout the nineties, Prosser served as the link between the trustees and ACS. He was crucial to the school's post-war recovery and growth.

The period of the Board's dislocation ended in 1997 when Sam Constan, the Board Chair and ACS alumnus, received special permission from the U.S. State Department to travel to Beirut.[25] His trip was quite an event. Constan met with Lebanon's Prime Minister, Rafic Hariri, held

Figure 10.6: Sam Constan '53, Chairman of the Board at ACS, during his visit to Beirut in 1997

three receptions for ACS faculty, staff, and parents, and spent a week visiting classes and meeting with administrators.[26] A year later, in June 1998, the ACS Board held its first post-war meeting in Beirut.[27] Prosser's efforts to maintain an active and engaged Board had paid off. Sadly, just a month later, Walter Prosser died in New York at the age of 76. In lieu of flowers, his family requested that donations be sent to the Walter Prosser Fund at ACS, the school that he had served with dedication for the last decade of his life.[28] This permanently endowed fund was established to award the Walter Prosser Graduation Prize to a student who with demonstrated academic distinction and commitment to the ACS Community Service Program.[29]

Both American and Lebanese

The Board of Trustees, while meeting in exile in New York, had affirmed ACS's wartime shift towards a dual identity. That affirmation was not necessarily a given as there was some pressure to return to an American-only school culture. But the Board recognized that there would be no return to the era of the "Golden American ghetto," and that to resist change would neither be possible nor wise. The first post-war change to the by-laws came in 1993, when the Board removed the Christian component of ACS's mission.[30] The new by-laws stated that ACS was a school within the "American non-sectarian tradition."[31] The term "non-sectarian" was especially poignant for a nation that had just survived

123

fifteen years of sectarian violence. The Board next updated its admissions policy. The school now sought to "enroll students without regards to race, creed, gender, national origin, or religious belief."[32] Gone was the policy that openly discouraged non-American applicants. Diversity, the school now believed, held inherent educational value. Finally, in 2001, the Board reaffirmed its dedication to both an American system of education and to the Lebanese Baccalaureate. While the school welcomed qualified students who "seek a rigorous American-style education," the Board wrote, it also "continues to explore the reconciliation of the American high school diploma requirements with the requirements of the Lebanese Ministry of Education."[33]

Figure 10.7: The science department in 1994

It fell on the shoulders of enthusiastic faculty to reconcile the differences between an American and a Lebanese education, to merge the two cultures, and to create a school that was half Lebanese and half American. Humanities teachers, teaching history and literature, worked to build fluency in English for students who spoke Arabic at home. Arabic teachers worked to build fluency in both formal and colloquial Arabic in students who had been raised overseas and had lost the language of their ancestors.[34] The history, science and math departments had to reconcile competing curricula – one required by the Lebanese government, the other approved by the National Association of Independent Schools, and later, a third required by the International Baccalaureate. The task may have seemed overwhelming in the difficult years immediately following the civil war. In response, ACS hired a remarkable group of young teachers who tackled the challenge with an idealism and energy that redefined the school, including a number of ACS graduates who came back to teach after the US ban on travel to Lebanon was lifted.

The New Generation of Teachers

The new teachers in the 1990s came of age during and were defined by the Lebanese Civil War. Considering the interruptions to their educations – from grade school through university – it is remarkable that this generation grew to be master teachers. As children, some fled Lebanon and adapted to foreign countries and cultures. Those who remained survived and adapted to extraordinary circumstances. Many changed schools several times due to school closures, the influence of militias, or other effects of the war. They did not receive the benefits of extracurricular activities, sports, fine arts, or outdoor education.[35] For many, their childhoods were confined to small neighborhoods in Beirut, which limited their movements to a few square city blocks.[36] Many also were educated in the French system, which emphasized discipline, lectures and memorization.[37] One teacher did not recall ever being encouraged, or even allowed, to ask questions.[38] Their educational experiences, of course, contrasted with the goals of the American Community School with its emphasis on creativity, independent thought, and student-centered learning. "None of my teachers was my role model," Rima Halabi, a first grade and later mathematics teacher, explained, expressing a sentiment common among the generation of teachers who grew up during the war.[39] These young teachers, who had endured extraordinary circumstances in childhood, were required to teach in an educational system that was foreign to them – to children who could not relate to their wartime experiences.

Figure 10.8: Haifa Hijazi

The administration therefore had to recruit the best and brightest young educators who were willing to experiment with a foreign style of teaching. The school leveraged its connection to AUB to recruit the most talented minds of the war generation. AUB delivered promising scientists, mathematicians, and education majors to ACS.[40] Rima Halabi got her job teaching first grade at ACS without applying for it: Halabi's mathematics professor, who recognized her talent, had sent Halabi's resume to the elementary school principal without asking for her permission.[41] Employment in Beirut was hard to find in the early 1990s and an ambitious graduate student at AUB could teach at ACS during the day, research a master's thesis at the University in the evening, and sleep in the Boarding Department at night.[42]

Figure 10.9: Students on field trip in 1994

ACS was committed to training its teachers to become American-style educators. The school held in-service training each week on Wednesdays with the goal of providing young teachers with alternatives to lecture-based classes.[43] "Those Wednesday trainings are how I learned to be a teacher," Viviane Khoury Saab remembered.[44] Likewise Khoury Saab's colleague in the science department, Dania Maaliki, became committed to student-centered learning in the early 1990s. "It was like a revelation," she explained. "I didn't know that teachers could be that cooperative and that helpful. I wanted to be that type of teacher who was 'nice' and engaged with her students."[45] When Suheir Sleiman, another science teacher, began her career at ACS, she realized how much she missed in her own education. "It was all memorization and I immediately forgot it," Sleiman said of her own years as a student. "I didn't remember students being allowed to participate and all of a sudden when I was in my twenties teaching at ACS I wanted to go back and do it all over."[46]

Managing the classroom at ACS in the early 1990s could be daunting for young teachers. Viviane Khoury Saab had to adjust to the new levels of maturity; she went from teaching graduate students to fifteen-year-olds.[47] In her first year at ACS, Dania Maaliki was a twenty-one year old teaching seventeen-year-old juniors. She questioned her ability to do it but she stayed with the job because of the encouragement of the high school principal.[48] Classrooms were lively, hyperactive places – in some ways, the students were products of a society lacking in structure after fifteen years of war.[49] Lina Daoud, a math teacher, recalled one section in which seven out of ten students were expelled for behavior issues.[50] Despite the rambunctiousness, students in the 1990s were earnest in their desires to improve their community. Students felt that they could make Belrut and the world a better place, and they organized campaigns to clean up their environment, to demand women's rights, to end cruelty to animals, and to change Lebanon's confessional politics.[51] Pent up idealism was unleashed among an energetic youth after the war, and the school's teachers fed off of that energy.

Figure 10.10: Student dance in the courtyard, 1997

The new generation of teachers needed the energy because their task was to recreate the school's programs from scratch. Teachers found new community service programs at orphanages and in refugee camps, and they then dedicated weekends to chaperoning student service trips.[52] Teachers had to learn how to raise money and to publish yearbooks – they found only one sponsor in 1992.[53] Teachers offered ballet, jazz, and computer courses for the first time. They organized short story contests, science fairs, and geological trips to Jordan. The librarians replaced worn, dusty books by organizing book drives and donations.[54] In the meantime, Bashshur guided the school through accreditation. ACS was the first English-speaking academic institution in Lebanon to obtain post-war accreditation. After this was received in 1993, the school began to move away from advanced placement courses towards the International Baccalaureate (IB) program, a shift in strategy long championed by Bashshur. The IB program was officially launched at ACS in 1995, and ACS was first in Lebanon to offer this program.

Much of the responsibility for complying with the accreditation process, the IB program, and the LB program was delegated to the teachers. Everyone was busy. Everyone had work to do. Most tackled their responsibilities with energy and with a sense of mission.

Teachers developed a strong sense of camaraderie. The faculty came from many areas of Lebanon and from different sectarian groups. But sectarianism did not enter the workplace. Bashshur delivered a clear message: ACS would be liberal, apolitical and secular. "We all wanted to rebuild the country and the school with it," remembers Wafa Kays. "ACS in the 1990s was an idealistic place. We had so much hope for the future."[55] Dania Maaliki believes that the hard work in recreating ACS may have been a product of a "survivor mentality" in which the teachers, having survived the war, had an insatiable desire to make up for lost time.[56] The students also recognized and participated in the special camaraderie. "The students, the teachers, the school – we were all growing together," explained Bana Abou Richeh '96. "Adults and students became really close. We were all trying to make it work and trying to revive ACS after a long period of decline."[57]

🌲

Catherine Bashshur stepped down as head of school in June 2003, two years before ACS celebrated its centennial. Bashshur had been a part of the school for nearly forty of those 100 years. When she began work at ACS in 1964 as a social studies teacher, the school was very much an American institution. In 1984, when she took over leadership, the school was on the verge of destruction. By the time that she retired in 2003, ACS was once again prospering – in enrollment, finances, and in the quality of its teachers, students and educational services. Bashshur did not save the school alone. In large part, the recovery was the result of the faculty hired by her – an outstanding core group of young teachers who were raised during the Lebanese Civil War and who remained at ACS after Bashshur's retirement. These teachers retained Bashshur's vision of ACS as a bi-cultural institution; by 2003, ACS was indeed both American and Lebanese.

Notes

[1] Bashshur, June 1992

[2] Bashshur, June 1992

[3] Bashshur, June 1994

[4] Sleiman [2012]

[5] ACS Board of Trustees, October 16, 1995

[6] Bedeir [2012]

[7] Bashshur, June 1992

[8] Maaliki [2012]

[9] Bashshur, June 1992

[10] ACS Board of Trustees, April 26, 1996

[11] Bedeir [2012]

[12] Bashshur, June 1992

[13] Madbak [2012]

[14] Stoops [1993]

[15] Stoops [1993]

[16] Abunnasr [2012]

[17] Obituary [1998]

[18] Abunnasr [2012]

[19] Prosser [1993a]

[20] ACS Board of Trustees, May 25, 1993

[21] Prosser [1993c]

[22] Prosser [1993b]

[23] Prosser [1995b]; Prosser [1993d]

[24] Prosser [1993e]; Prosser [1996]; Prosser [1995a]

[25] ACS Board of Trustees, April 21, 1997

[26] Constan [1997]

[27] ACS Board of Trustees, June 18, 1998

[28] Obituary [1998]

[29] ACS [2011]

[30] ACS Board of Trustees, March 16, 2001

[31] ACS Board of Trustees [1993]

[32] ACS Board of Trustees, June 18, 1998

[33] ACS Board of Trustees [2001]

[34] Kays [2012]

[35] Sleiman [2012]

[36] Madbak [2012]

[37] Abdallah [2012]

[38] Daoud [2012b]

[39] Halabi [2012]

[40] Bashshur, June 1994

[41] Halabi [2012]

[42] Khoury Saab [2012]

[43] Bashshur, June 1992

[44] Khoury Saab [2012]

[45] Maaliki [2012]

[46] Sleiman [2012]

[47] Khoury Saab [2012]

[48] Maaliki [2012]

[49] Madbak [2012]

[50] Daoud [2012a]

[51] Madbak [2012]

[52] Khoury Saab [2012]

[53] ACS [d, 1992]

[54] Jawhary [2012]

[55] Kays [2012]

[56] Maaliki [2012]

[57] Abou Richeh [2005]

11 Epilogue: The Summer of 2006

Dr. George Damon became head of school in the fall of 2003, bringing with him a long career in education. He had previously served as a head of school in Izmir, Turkey, principal at Robert College in Istanbul, and as a professor in Massachusetts.[1] "I acquired a rebuilt school in 2003," Damon explained. "We had 1,015 students. We were then at the peak of the reconstruction under Rafic Hariri. Everything was positive. The school was a vibrant place."[2] Events in Lebanon, however, soon challenged Damon's leadership.

The challenge began in early 2005. During the school's 100th year, former Prime Minister Rafic Hariri was assassinated. "We were expecting Lebanon to return to an era of politics by assassination," Damon said later.[3] That spring, nearly a fifth of the school's students temporarily withheld their reenrollment contracts for the upcoming year.[4] Yet the school moved forward, and it refused to cancel the planned centennial celebration. About 100 alumni returned to the school that June, despite the political situation, in what Damon described as a "euphoric celebration."[5] By the fall of 2005, enrollment had climbed back to over 1,000, a record number of alumni donated to the centennial campaign, and politics seemed to be settling back to normal.[6] By the spring and summer of 2006, Lebanon was preparing for a record year in tourism.[7] Damon travelled to Turkey in early July for his summer vacation.

Then, on July 12, 2006, after months of rising tensions, war broke out between Israel and Hezbollah. A core group of staff and administrators was on the way to work that summer morning. Mony Kfoury, an administrative assistant, was walking to school after picking up some manaeesh from Faysal's when she heard the news. She was planning to meet Guitta Bayouk, another assistant, to clean out the high school files. The files, and all of the other summer projects, would have to wait.[8] The war erupted in the south, in Dahieh[9], and in the Bekaa Valley. Ras Beirut remained eerily quiet. Construction projects fell silent. Parking lots along Hamra were empty and stores were closed. Robert Easton,

131

an ACS teacher, kept a blog and recorded his observations at the time, "So much of what we see [in Ras Beirut] seems normal... Then we hear the jets and the explosions and we know that our time in Hamra is an illusion of normalcy." Easton added, on July 19, "The school is quiet. The guards are all there."[10]

The war lasted 34 days. It resulted in billions of dollars of destruction to homes, factories, and to the nation's infrastructure. It led to the flight of 1.6 million tourists, the movement of roughly a million refugees from southern Lebanon, and the death of approximately 1,200 Lebanese citizens.[11]

A lot of effort went into keeping ACS safe during the 34 days of war. Ibrahim Bedeir, head of the physical plant, moved his entire staff – 28 people – onto campus and into faculty housing. Many of the staff lived in areas directly affected by the bombing, and their presence in faculty housing kept them safe and also deterred break-ins. The faculty lounge became a temporary dorm, with staff spending the night in sleeping bags and on mattresses. "The camaraderie was great," Bedeir remembers. "I was really impressed by our physical plant staff at that moment."[12]

Meanwhile, George Damon, who was stranded in rural Turkey, was in phone contact with his administration on a daily basis. Middle School Principal Karim Abu Haydar, Director of Development Fadwa Ghannoum, Business Manager Fadi Germanos, and Director of Admissions Najwa Zabad were in Beirut and in action at the school.[13] Damon and his team reported to the Board of Trustees every five days by conference call. By the end of July, local trustees speculated that the war might be a prolonged one. The administrative team discussed the possibility of running out of fuel and the potential that ACS might be overrun with refugees.[14] Some members of the Board, having lived through the Civil War, anticipated the shelling of central Beirut. As the war continued into early August, administrators in Beirut worked on the logistics of providing power, leading staff meetings, and quelling rumors that the school would close for the year. The Development Office contacted alumni to solicit emergency funding which began to arrive before the war ended.[15] In the meantime, Damon was struggling in Damascus to obtain a visa to enter Lebanon.[16] At 7:30 a.m., a few hours after the ceasefire was declared on August 14, Damon reentered Lebanon from the north Bekaa Valley entry point. He drove past bombed out bridges, craters, and destroyed vehicles, and reached ACS late that evening.

After arriving, Damon faced two questions: (1) how many students would ACS have in the fall and (2) how many teachers were required to meet the needs of those students?[17] The answer to the first was unclear. During the war, only 200-300 families were able to communicate with ACS and to commit to attending in the fall. In mid-August, Damon and the Board predicted at least a 40 percent drop in enrollment for the upcoming year. Then, gradually, the school regained contact with its families. Teachers such as Wafa Kays worked with the Development Office in a phone bank, calling overseas to inform families that ACS would be open for business. The school then committed to a start date: October 3. This would allow time for the airport, heavily damaged during the war, to be repaired and families to make arrangements to return. "When we finally got back in touch with our families," Damon recalled, "most said of course we're coming back. That's what Lebanon is all about. You have a disturbance. You make sure that you're safe and then you go and put your life back together." By the opening day of school, 914 students attended. ACS had expected only 600.[18]

In the interim, Damon had to deal with the second question – how many teachers to rehire. On the one hand, he did not want to guarantee jobs and then lay off faculty during the school year. On the other hand, Damon did not want to lose some of ACS's finest teachers. He concluded that the correct decision was transparency. He notified teachers during the war that faculty would be rehired in the fall based on the needs dictated by enrollment. He could not guarantee employment, Damon warned, and teachers might need to look elsewhere for a job. For many faculty, this potential loss of employment was as traumatic as the summer war.[19] The result was a 25 percent loss in the faculty – both local and foreign – that fall.[20]

ACS moved forward in 2006 and 2007, as it had through a hundred years of change and conflict. Mony Kfoury, a member of the staff who helped the school survive that summer, reflected that "Closing is never on the table. We don't know what will happen but we know that ACS will stay open."[21] George Damon said, "We are the foundation of our community in a moment of crisis. ACS has to act as a pillar for people to wrap themselves around."[22]

Since the conflict of 2006, Beirut and ACS have enjoyed growth and relative prosperity – especially in light of the "Great Recession" that has gripped the United States and Europe. Lebanon is witnessing the Arab Spring in some of the nearby countries. In particular, it has an uneasy eye on the crises in Syria and on threats between Israel and

Iran. Regional instability is not new to Lebanon, Beirut or ACS. Since 1905, Beirut and ACS have never enjoyed any lasting tranquility. But the American Community School at Beirut has consistently responded to every challenge with a singular purpose: ACS will adapt and survive. And, in doing so, it will deliver excellence in education.

Notes

[1] ACS [d, 2004]

[2] Damon [2012]

[3] Damon [2012]

[4] ACS Board of Trustees, April 26, 2005

[5] ACS Board of Trustees, June 18, 2005

[6] ACS Board of Trustees, July 3, 2005

[7] Damon [2012]

[8] Kfoury [2012]

[9] Beirut's southern suburbs, commonly understood as Haret Hreyk and surroundings, where Hizbullah's institutions are located.

[10] ACS [d, 2007]

[11] ACS [d, 2007]

[12] Bedeir [2012]

[13] ACS Board of Trustees, July 26, 2006

[14] ACS Board of Trustees, July 26, 2006

[15] ACS Board of Trustees, August 2, 2006

[16] Damon [2012]

[17] Damon [2012]

[18] Damon [2012]

[19] Alamuddin [2012]

[20] Damon [2012]

[21] Kfoury [2012]

[22] Damon [2012]

Bibliography

Akram Abdallah. Email to the author, May 7 2012.

Aberystwyth University. "General Registry of Graduates". Aberystwyth University, Aberystwyth, October 2011. URL http://archives.ulrls.lon.ac.uk/resources/general_register_part_3.pdf.

Bana Abou Richeh. Interview by ACS Development Office. Transcribed from video recording, ACS archives, Beirut, April 21 2005.

Maria Bashshur Abunnasr. Interview by ACS Development Office. Transcribed from video recording, ACS archives, Beirut, April 27 2005.

Maria Bashshur Abunnasr. Email to the author, May 8 2012.

ACS. *ACS Handbook.* American Community School, Beirut, a.

ACS. *Yearbook.* American Community School, Beirut, b.

ACS. *Al Arz.* American Community School, ACS Archives, Beirut, c.

ACS. *Al Manara Yearbook.* American Community School, Beirut, d.

ACS. *Echo Newsletter.* American Community School, ACS Archives, Beirut, e.

ACS. *ACS Newsletter.* American Community School, Beirut, f.

ACS. *The American Community School Idea in Beirut, Syria.* American Community School, ACS Archives, Beirut, 1923.

ACS. *ACS Curriculum, 1961-1962.* ACS Archives, Beirut, 1961a.

ACS. *ACS Bulletin of Information.* ACS Archives, Beirut, 1961b.

ACS. *ACS Brochure.* ACS Archives, Beirut, 1963.

ACS. *Questionnaire for Parents.* ACS Archives, Beirut, 1964.

ACS. *ACS Brochure.* ACS Archives, Beirut, 1966-1967.

ACS. *1967 Awards Program.* ACS Archives, Beirut, 1967.

ACS. "ACS List of Endowed Funds". American Community School, 2011. URL http://www.acs.edu.lb/page.cfm?p=588.

ACS Board of Trustees. *By-laws of the American Community School.* ACS Archives, Beirut.

ACS Board of Trustees. *Minutes of Board Meetings.* American Community School, Beirut.

ACS Board of Trustees. "Final Draft of Revised By-Laws for American Community School.". ACS Archives, September 30 1993.

ACS Board of Trustees. "The Strategic Plan of the American Community School at Beirut". ACS Archives, March 2001.

al Jumhuriyah al-Lubnaniyah al-Jaridah al Rasmiyah al. Decree number 5262, September 20 1988.

Laila Faris Alamuddin. Interview by ACS Development Office. Transcribed from a video recording, ACS archives, Beirut, April 22 2004.

Laila Faris Alamuddin. Email to Patricia Buckley, November 28 2012.

Nada Aoun. Interview by the author. Transcribed from MP3 recording, March 2 2012.

JoAnn Atwood. Interview by ACS Development Office. Transcribed from video recording, ACS archives, Beirut, February 23 2005.

AUB. Aub photograph collection. Jafet Library, Archives and Special Collections Department, AUB, 18-1900s.

AUB. Howard Bliss Personal Collection. Jafet Library, Archives and Special Collections Department, AUB, 1900s.

Rae Azkoul. Interview by ACS Development Office. Transcribed from a video recording, ACS archives, Beirut, April 27 2005.

David Bailey. Autobiography in song. In Anne Peet Carrington and Børre Ludvigsen, editors, *When... not if,* Stories of Conflicts in the Middle East. Al Mashriq, 2010. ISBN 978-82-999320-0-4.

Deirdre Ball. Interview by ACS Development Office. Transcribed from video recording, ACS archives, Beirut.

Karl Barbir. "ACS Commencement Address". ACS archives, June 17 1966.

Catherine Bashshur. *State of School.* ACS Archives.

Catherine Bashshur. Interview by the author. Transcribed from MP3 recording, February 29 2012.

Catherine Carlin Bashshur. Interview by ACS Development Office. Transcribed from a video recording, ACS archives, Beirut, April 27 2005.

Ibrahim Bedeir. Interview by the author. Transcribed from MP3 recording, May 4 2012.

Daniel Bliss. *Two Worlds Apart: An American's Intimate Account of Growing Up in the Arab World of 1902-1923*. Monmouth Press, Monmouth, Maine, 2003.

Howard Bliss. Letter to Bayard Dodge. AUB Archives, Howard Bliss Collection, November 2 1907.

Howard Bliss. Letter to David Stuart Dodge. AUB Archives, Howard Bliss Collection, Octorber 2 1914.

Howard Bliss. Letter to David Stuart Dodge. AUB Archives, Howard Bliss Collection, March 22 1917a.

Howard Bliss. Letter to Alfred E. Day. AUB Archives, Howard Bliss Collection, November 1 1917b.

Howard Bliss. Letter to W.D.P. Bliss. AUB Archives, Howard Bliss Collection, September 10 1917c.

Howard Bliss. Letter to David Stuart Dodge. AUB Archives, Howard Bliss Collection, March 22 1917d.

Howard Bliss. Letter to C.F. Gates. AUB Archives, Howard Bliss Collection, October 24 1917e.

Howard Bliss. Letter to David Stuart Dodge. AUB Archives, Howard Bliss Collection, July 23 1917f.

Howard Bliss. Letter to David Stuart Dodge. AUB Archives, Howard Bliss Collection, May 5 1917g.

Howard Bliss. Letter to W.D.P. Bliss. AUB Archives, Howard Bliss Collection, December 12 1917h.

Board of Trustees of the Syrian Protestant College. *Minutes of Board Meetings*. Syrian Protestant College, Beirut.

Maysa Boubess. Interview by the author. Transcribed from MP3 recording, March 1 2012.

Anna Boustany. Interview by the author. Transcribed from MP3 recording, March 2 2012.

Captain Brickhouse, A.A. Jr. "Tapline's Sidon Terminal". *World Petroleum*, reprint, June 1957.

Sanborn C. Brown. *Everyday Stories, Tales of a Beirut Boyhood*. Mayio Design, W. Lebanon, NH, 2006.

Marianne Buckley. Interview by the author. Transcribed from MP3 recording, March 19 2012.

William R. Chandler. "The Growing Years of the American Community School". Speech to parents association, ACS archives, Beirut, December 6 1963.

Jeremy Chapman. Interview by the author. Transcribed from notes, February 26 2012.

William Cleveland. *A History of the Modern Middle East*. Westview Press, Oxford, 2004. ISBN 978-0813340487.

Cochran. Letters from Beirut, 1937-1939.

Ivy Cleo Compton-Bishop. Interview by Ibtissam Saadawi. Transcribed from a video recording, ACS archives, Beirut, December 22 1996.

Quentin Compton-Bishop. Email to the author, April 9 2012.

Sam Constan. Memo to the Board of Trustees. ACS Archives, May 12 1997.

Sam Constan. Interview. Transcribed from video recording, ACS archives, Beirut, February 26 2005.

Archibald Stuart Crawford. Letter to Mrs. Abdu Barbir. ACS Archives, April 27 1972a.

Archibald Stuart Crawford. *Evacuations of Americans from Beirut, 1828-1967*. Librairie du Liban, Beirut, 1972b.

George Damon. Interview by the author. Transcribed from MP3 recording, May 17 2012.

Lina Daoud. Interview by the author. Transcribed from MP3 recording, May 4 2012a.

Lina Daoud. Email to the author, May 13 2012b.

Philip Davies. Interview by ACS Development Office. Transcribed from video recording, ACS archives, Beirut, September 11 2004.

Bayard Dodge. Letter to Mrs. Cleveland Dodge. The Bayard Dodge Collection, AUB Archives, January 7 1941a.

Bayard Dodge. Letter to Albert W. Staub. The Bayard Dodge Collection, AUB Archives, July 15 1941b.

Bayard Dodge. Letter to son. The Bayard Dodge Collection, AUB Archives, October 27 1943.

Bayard Dodge. *The American University of Beirut: A Brief History of the University and the Lands which it Serves.* Khayat's, Beirut, 1958.

Ebba El-Hage. Interview by ACS Development Office. Transcribed from video recording, ACS archives, Beirut.

Malek el Jisr. 12th grade skip day. In Anne Peet Carrington and Børre Ludvigsen, editors, *When... not if,* Stories of Conflicts in the Middle East. Al Mashriq, 2010. ISBN 978-82-999320-0-4.

Laila Farah. Interview by ACS Development Office. Transcribed from video recording, ACS archives, Beirut, November 12 2004.

Elisabeth West FitzHugh. *"Thoughts on ACS, 1932-1941".* ACS Archives.

Elisabeth West FitzHugh. Interview by ACS Development Office. Transcribed from video recording, ACS archives, Beirut, July 22 2004.

Thomas L Friedman. *From Beirut to Jerusalem.* Farrar, Straus, Giroux, New York, 1st edition, 1989. ISBN 0374158940.

Grace Dodge Guthrie. *Legacy to Lebanon.* G.D. Guthrie, Richmond, Va., 1984.

Rima Halabi. Email to the author, May 8 2012.

Pril Dorman Hall. Pril Dorman Hall Private Collection. 1920s.

Rachel Hall. *Memoirs.* Handwritten memoirs, 2001.

Ronnie Hammad. Interview by ACS Development Office. Transcribed from video recording, ACS archives, Beirut.

Linda Handschin-Sheppard. Interview by ACS Development Office. Transcribed from video recording, ACS archives, Beirut, November 24 2004.

Haifa Hijazi. Interview by the author. Transcribed from MP3 recording, February 28 2012.

Heidi Hilgendorf. Interview by ACS Development Office. Transcribed from a video recording, ACS archives, Beirut, July 11 2004.

Barea Jawhary. Interview by the author. Transcribed from MP3 recording, May 4 2012.

Eleanor Dorman Johnson. Interview by ACS Development Office. Transcribed from video recording, ACS archives, Beirut, April 22 2005.

Samir Kassir. *Beirut*. University of California Press, Berkeley, 2010. ISBN 9780520256682.

Wafa Kays. Interview by the author. Transcribed from MP3 recording, May 4 2012.

Mony Kfoury. Interview by the author. Transcribed from MP3 recording, May 17 2012.

Samir Khalaf. *Heart of Beirut: Reclaiming the Bourj*. Saqi Books, London, 2006.

Viviane Khoury Saab. Interview by the author. Transcribed from MP3 recording, May 4 2012.

Margaret Bliss Leavitt. Letter to Wilfred Turmelle. ACS Archives, September 2 1972a.

Margaret Bliss Leavitt. Letter to Wilfred Turmelle. ACS Archives, June 28 1972b.

Margaret Bliss Leavitt. Letter to Elisabeth West FitzHugh, September 11 1980. Transcribed and emailed to the author by Allen West, November 1 2011.

Annabel Lee. "UPS: Professor Recalls Middle East Turmoil". *The Tacoma News Tribune and Sunday Ledger*, June 9 1968.

Christian Lund. Interview by ACS Development Office. Transcribed from video recording, ACS archives, Beirut, November 28 2004.

Dania Maaliki. Interview by the author. Transcribed from MP3 recording, May 4 2012.

Samer Madbak. Interview by the author. Transcribed from MP3 recording, May 4 2012.

Eric Matson. Matson photograph collection. Library of Congress Prints and Photographs Division, LOC, 1898-1946.

Marvin McFeaters. Interview by ACS Development Office. Transcribed from video recording, ACS archives, Beirut, September 9 2004.

Marvin McFeaters. Interview by ACS Development Office. Transcribed from video recording, ACS archives, Beirut, September 20 2005.

Margaret Merrill. Letter to Daddy. Private collection of Pril Dorman Hall, November 15 1925a.

Margaret Merrill. Letter to Mumsie and Daddy. Private collection of Pril Dorman Hall, October 31 1925b.

Margaret Merrill. Letter to Daddy. Private collection of Pril Dorman Hall, May 7 1925c.

Margaret Merrill. Letter to Mother. Private collection of Pril Dorman Hall, June 1 1925d.

Margaret Merrill. Letter to Mother and Daddy. Private collection of Pril Dorman Hall, February 15 1925e.

Margaret Merrill. Letter to Mother. Private collection of Pril Dorman Hall, October 16 1925f.

Margaret Merrill. Letter to Mother. Private collection of Pril Dorman Hall, April 5 1925g.

Margaret Merrill. Letter to Mother and Daddy. Private collection of Pril Dorman Hall, June 1926.

Dorothy Merrill Dorman. Letter to Margaret. Private collection of Pril Dorman Hall, December 7 1926.

Nadia Mihdahi. Interview by ACS Development Office. Transcribed from video recording, ACS archives, Beirut, April 22 2005.

Craig Miller. Interview by ACS Development Office. Transcribed from video recording, ACS archives, Beirut, November 24 2004.

Franklin Moore. Moore photograph collection. Jafet Library, Archives and Special Collections Department, AUB, 1892-1905.

Howard Neff. Memo to John Kelberer. ACS Archives, Unknown year.

Edward Nickolay. Edward Nickolay to David Stuart Dodge. AUB Archives, Edward Nickolay Collection, December 11 1919.

Edward Nickolay. Edward Nickolay to David Stuart Dodge. AUB Archives, Edward Nickolay Collection, January 20 1920.

John Nohos. Interview by the author. Transcribed from MP3 recording, March 7 2012.

Obituary. "The Death of Howard Bliss". *Al-Kulliyeh*, (AUB Archives, Howard Bliss Collection), VI(11), July 1920a.

Obituary. Howard S. Bliss. *Newsletter from Robert College*, (AUB Archives, Howard Bliss Collection), 1(3), June 1920b.

Obituary. Amy Blatchford Bliss. *Near East Quarterly,* (AUB Archives 7/2), 2(3), 1941.

Obituary. "Paid Notice: Deaths – PROSSER, WALTER R.". *The New York Times,* July 18 1998.

Stephen B. L Penrose. *That they may have life: the story of the American University of Beirut, 1866-1941.* Trustees of the American University of Beirut, New York, 1941.

Barbara Porter. Interview by ACS Development Office. Transcribed from video recording, ACS archives, Beirut, March 11 2004.

Walter Prosser. Letter to Dr. John Stoops. ACS Archives, May 23 1993a.

Walter Prosser. Memo to Munir Khalidy. ACS Archives, October 28 1993b.

Walter Prosser. Memo to the Board of Trustees. ACS Archives, June 17 1993c.

Walter Prosser. Letter to Mr. Michael Daher, Ministry of Education. ACS Archives, May 25 1993d.

Walter Prosser. Letter to Mr. Nadim Munla. ACS Archives, May 26 1993e.

Walter Prosser. Letter to Miss Dina Dabbous. ACS Archives, October 16 1995a.

Walter Prosser. Memo to the Board of Trustees. ACS Archives, October 3 1995b.

Walter Prosser. Letter to Yahya Farhat. ACS Archives, April 17 1996.

Leslie Rogers. Interview by ACS Development Office. Transcribed from video recording, ACS archives, Beirut, November 11 2004.

Ray Ruehl. "The Beginning of the Civil War". In Anne Peet Carrington and Børre Ludvigsen, editors, *When... not if,* Stories of Conflicts in the Middle East. Al Mashriq, 2010. ISBN 978-82-999320-0-4.

Belle Dorman Rugh. "First Day of School". *The Diaspora Potrezebie,* XIII (4), December 1991.

Bob Samuel. Interview by ACS Development Office. Transcribed from video recording, ACS archives, Beirut, November 18 2004.

Sarrafian. Sarrafian photograph collection. Jafet Library, Archives and Special Collections Department, AUB, 1900s.

Mary-Averett Seelye. Interview by ACS Development Office. Transcribed from a video recording, ACS Archives, November 7 2004.

Agnes Shamma. Interview by ACS Development Office. Transcribed from video recording, ACS archives, Beirut, April 22 2005.

Suheir Sleiman. Interview by the author. Transcribed from MP3 recording, May 4 2012.

Jon Stacey, editor. *A History of the American Community School at Beirut*. Alumni Association of the American Community School at Beirut, Beirut, 1997.

Jon Stacey. Interview by ACS Development Office. Transcribed from a video recording, ACS archives, Beirut, November 21 2005.

George B. Steward. Letter to Albert W. Staub. The Bayard Dodge Collection, AUB Archives, June 14 1941.

Dr. John Stoops. *The Report of an Evaluation of the American Community School, Beirut, Lebanon.* The Commission on Elementary Schools of the Middle States Association of Colleges and Schools, ACS Archives, April 1993.

The Record. *The Record Newsletter.* American Community School, Beirut.

Elizabeth Thompson. *Colonial citizens: republican rights, paternal privilege, and gender in French Syria and Lebanon.* The history and society of the modern Middle East. Columbia University Press, New York, 2000. ISBN 0231106602.

William Tracy. "A Reunion in Boston". *Aramco World Magazine,* 40(4), July-August 1989.

William Tracy. Interview by ACS Development Office. Transcribed from a video recording, ACS archives, Beirut, December 12 2004.

Charlotte Ward. Ward papers. Mount Holyoke College Archives and Special Collections, 1899-1973. URL http://mtholyoke.cdmhost.com/cdm/singleitem/collection/p1030coll8/id/5561/rec/18.

Charlotte Ward. Letter to Home People. Mount Holyoke Archives and Special Collections, November 14 1914.

Charlotte Ward. Letter to Home People. Mount Holyoke Archives and Special Collections, April 5 1915.

Charlotte Ward. Letter to Home People. Mount Holyoke Archives and Special Collections, February 18 1920.

Charlotte Ward. Letter to Home People. Mount Holyoke Archives and Special Collections, April 16 1923a.

Charlotte Ward. Letter to Home People. Mount Holyoke Archives and Special Collections, August 23 1923b.

Charlotte Ward. Letter to Home People. Mount Holyoke Archives and Special Collections, August 13 1923c.

Charlotte Ward. Letter to Esther and Paul. Mount Holyoke Archives and Special Collections, December 13 1926a.

Charlotte Ward. Letter to Home People. Mount Holyoke Archives and Special Collections, October 16 1926b.

Charlotte Ward. Letter to Paul. Mount Holyoke Archives and Special Collections, December 18 1927.

Allen West. Email to Fadwa Ghannoum. ACS Archives, December 3 2010.

Allen West. Email to the author, October 28 2011a.

Dorothy West. Letters to her children, October 1949. Transcribed and emailed to the author by David West, November 28 2011b.

William West. Letter to Dorothy West, June 25 1946. Transcribed and emailed to the author by David West, November 28 2011c.

David Williams. Interview by ACS Development Office. Transcribed from a video recording, ACS archives, Beirut, November 18 2004.

Pieter Wybro. Interview by ACS Development Office. Transcribed from video recording, ACS archives, Beirut, November 15 2004.

Najwa Zabad. Interview by ACS Development Office. Transcribed from video recording, ACS archives, Beirut.

Helen Zughaib. Interview by ACS Development Office. Transcribed from video recording, ACS archives, Beirut, September 11 2004.

A Appendices

Principals and heads of school

1905-1916	Winifred Thornton
1916-1919	Margaret Bliss '11
1919-1921	Elizabeth Jessup
1921-1924	Winifred Rouse
1924-1928	Margaret Ritsher
1928-1929	Violet Bender
1930-1932	Rhoda Orme
1932-1933	Eleanor Ireland Dickerman
1933-1940	Rhoda Orme
1940-1941	Curtis Strong
1941-1945	Ivy Cleo de Gorkiewicz '35
1945-1951	Richard S. Ford
1951-1952	Ashley T. Day
1952-1956	T. Robert Bassett
1956-1959	Clarence Schultz
1959-1960	F. Laurence White
1960-1965	Dwight E. Knox
1965-1971	Jack H. Harrison
1971-1979	W. Robert Usellis
1979-1984	Elsa Turmelle
1984-2003	Catherine C. Bashshur
2003-2013	George Damon
2013-	Hamilton Clark

Timeline

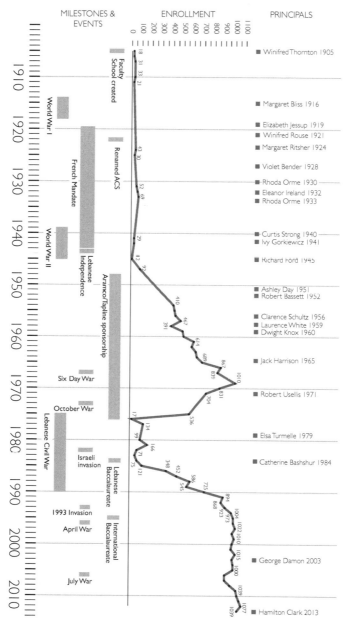

Figure A.1: Timeline of important events, enrollment, and heads of school.

Corniche campus

Figure A.2: By the late 1960s ACS's campus on the Corniche was complete. Here seen from one of Tapline's DC-3 aircraft approaching Beirut Airport.

149

Maps

Figure A.3: West Beirut, showing the main locations of ACS

150

Figure A.4: Lebanon with borders after the 1967 war.

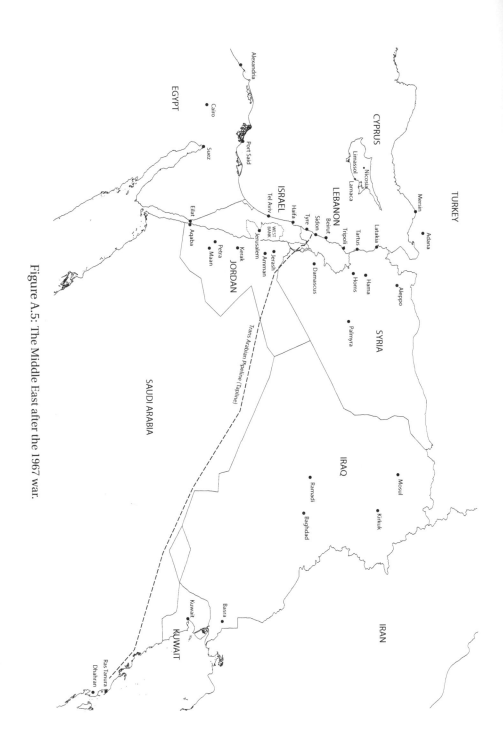

Figure A.5: The Middle East after the 1967 war.

Index

155

157

158

This book was typeset with the LATEX system created by Leslie Lamport, using Peter Wilson's memoir class. The body text is set 10pt on a 33pc measure with Computer Modern Roman designed by Donald Knuth, the inventor of the TEX typesetting system for "making beautiful books".

Wade Hampton Morris, Jr.

On graduating from the Lovett School in Atlanta, Georgia, at the turn of the millenium, Wade Morris went to study history at the University of Virginia where he received a BA majoring in the roots of contemporary Russia.

After a short program on the modern intricacies of teaching at Columbia University in 2008, he entered Georgetown University where he received his MA in liberal studies specializing in "Democracy in America: In Practice and Theory" and the integration of Episcopal secondary schools in the 1960s.

From 2004, Wade taught high school classes in history at The Collegiate School, Richmond, VA and St. Stephen's & St. Agnes School, Alexandria, VA, before coming to Beirut in 2009.

At the American Community School at Beirut, Wade taught world history covering the 15th century through WWI. In addition to researching and writing *A History of ACS*, he organized and ran a number of workshops, seminars, and mentoring programs for both colleagues and students, including teaching English as a volunteer at the Bourj el-Barajne Palestinian Camp women's center.

The Morris family, including daughters Jane (who was born in Beirut) and Annie, are now back in Atlanta, Georgia – where Wade is teaching at the Lovett School.